THE MAGPIE CAFE

Cook Book

"I cook with wine. Sometimes I even add it to the food" *WC Fields*

"There is no love sincerer than the love of good food" *George Bernard Shaw*

The Magpie Café

Cook Book

recipes inspired by the North Yorkshire coast

Foreword

by Brian Turner, CBE

If my mom was still around, in fact my dad an'all, they would be really chuffed to know that I have been asked to write a foreword to the Magpie's first cookery book. It is a number of years now since I last visited the Magpie and I had such a great time, standing in this rather long queue, the sun beating on my head and after at least half an hour, which seemed like two hours, of anticipation and banter, I was fed what can only be termed God's food.

Being brought up in the industrial West Riding I consider I have been privileged to sample so many differing styles of fish and chips, that even now whenever I venture into a new shop, no matter where it is in the country, I have to give them the Turner test. Is it cod or is it haddock, is it skin on or skin off, no bones, hot chips, crispy batter, malt vinegar and real salt... all for me are the true test of fish and chips. So welcome to this, their first book of recipes that all contribute to the main event of the Magpie.

Truly a champion of foods served in a champion fashion - I wish I was there now.

Enjoy some for me!

Dedicated to Ian and Sheila McKenzie,
without whom none of this would have been possible.
Also, our loyal staff and customers, who have helped over
the years to make The Magpie what it is today.

Thanks to Wayne Gildroy, Marie Paling, Lou Middlemas,
Philip Coverdale and Duncan Robson for their help in
preparing the dishes and keeping the show running
whilst we were busy playing at being authors.

Thanks to our fish merchant Dennis Crooks,
Bub Noble(R.J Noble), Chris at Pagendam Pratt Wines,
Bob Marsden, Harry Collet, Alan Whitworth
and Brian Turner C.B.E for their help in making this book.

Ian and Paul would also like to thank their long suffering partners
Elaine and Lindsay for all their uncomplaining help,
missed days off and late night-early morning typing
and proof reading sessions.

THE MAGPIE CAFE

Cook Book

Published on behalf of the Magpie Café by:

REGIONAL MAGAZINE COMPANY
DELIVERING QUALITY SINCE 1986

5 Broadfield Court
Broadfield Business Park
Sheffield S8 0XF
Tel: 0114 250 6300 Fax: 0114 250 6320
martin.edwards@regionalmagazine.co.uk

Photography:
Peter Goulding, f-eleven photography
0114 262 1048

Additional contributors:
Martin Edwards, Nigel Aplin, Linda Robbins

Design:
Michael Naylor, Paul Cocker

With special thanks to Brian Turner CBE

contents

About the authors

Ian Robson was born and still lives in Whitby. He worked in the plastics industry before making a life-changing decision to embark on a career in pursuit of his first love, good food. Initially working for the then owners, he arrived at The Magpie in 1980. Eventually taking over the business on their retirement in 1990 he continued to build on the Magpie's reputation and create the world-famous institution it is today. He remains actively involved in the running of the café on a daily basis, but finds time to pursue his other passion, Newcastle United. A devoted fan of the club appropriately nicknamed the Magpies. His quieter moments are spent around the North Yorkshire coastline with his camera.

Paul Gildroy is the driving force behind the Magpie Café's 'engine room'. As head chef, he presides over the kitchens which produce food so good that diners will frequently queue for an hour just to sample it. After school in Whitby, he learned the catering trade in nearby Scarborough before returning to his home town, and its best-known restaurant. It was a return to familiar surroundings in more ways than one - Paul can claim an association with the Magpie Café dating back to the days when, as a 12-year-old, he got his first job - buttering bread. His firm belief in allowing the simple natural flavours of good fresh ingredients to prevail, rather than detracting from them by complicated cooking techniques, has won over customers and critics alike. He lives with his family in Whitby, often accompanying Ian to Newcastle United matches.

Introduction

There is no mistaking The Magpie Café; the gleaming white building stands majestically overlooking the harbour on Whitby's Pier Road, revelling in its reputation as a Mecca for visitors to the town and the place where the locals go to get the best fish and chips in the north of England.

The Magpie has been described as the seafood lovers' paradise and people come from all over the world to sit in the famous bay window overlooking the North Sea looking up towards the 199 steps to the Abbey beyond.

Old pictures show that The Magpie has been on Pier Road since the 1900s, although it didn't actually move to number 14 until 1939. - current owner Ian Robson found an inscribed piece of wood saying so when he was carrying out alterations last year.

But the building has a much richer history dating back almost three centuries, which reflects the social and economic changes in Whitby over the years.

According to local historian Alan Whitworth it was built in the 1720s probably as a speculative venture. It fronted on to The Crag - a street named after the cliff face nearby - with the back of the house facing the quayside. There were perhaps as many as 200 houses on both sides of the street, owned by the lower middle classes of the time - like shop keepers and ship's captains.

Then, in the 1760s there was a major landslide when part of the cliff came crashing down demolishing most of the houses on one side of the street. As a result the remaining houses were remodelled and turned round to face the harbour and a new promenade was created. The building where The Magpie stands today was given its smart new bay windows - the first bay windows to feature in Whitby - and became home to a member of the celebrated Scoresby family.

William Scoresby senior was, for many years, the most prolific whaler in Europe. He was a brave entrepreneur with a swashbuckling side to his character; on one of his many trips to the

frozen north, he successfully saw off an enemy ship lurking off the Yorkshire coast. His son, William junior, who went to sea at the age of 14 and went on to command the family-owned ship The Fame, reputedly lived in the house.

In the 19th century the area around the promenade began to decline. The building which was to become The Magpie Café ceased to be a family home and was taken over as Whitby's Pilotage. It was the place where the shipping pilots would meet the sea captains and discuss navigating a safe passage into and out of the harbour.

Towards the end of the century, Albert Harrowing - owner of Harrowings Shipping Company, then the third largest shipping company in the country - bought the building and turned it into a shipping office.

Harrowings Shipping Company was a well-respected business and Albert, who lived in a fine country home in Aislaby, was a canny businessman. According to Whitby's psychic specialist and historian, Harry Collett, he would sit upstairs in the top office of the building and watch his boats come in. When they were a few miles off shore, sailors would be sent over the side to paint the starboard side of the boat so that when it arrived in port it would appear to be in pristine condition. Albert would point this out to potential clients and tell them: "You can see how we look after our ships and we would look after your cargo just as well."

Harry Collett reckons it was this which spawned the phrase 'there's a right way to do something, there's a wrong way and there's the Whitby way!'

Gradually shipping declined and Harrowings closed the Whitby office and concentrated on the London base. Originally next to the old lifeboat station, The Magpie relocated before ending up at number 14 Pier Road shortly before the Second World War.

Whitby Historian: Harry Collett

The McKenzie family became involved in the business in the 1950s. Ian McKenzie ran a fish and chip shop in Church Street and - for just a year in 1954 - he ran The Magpie Café too. But it was just too much to manage both and in 1955 his father-in-law Clifford Barker, a former estate agent, came out of retirement to take on the job with his wife Gladys.

When the couple retired again in 1965 son-in-law Ian and his wife Sheila sold the fish and chip shop in Church Street and took over The Magpie.

In those days fish and chip shops had a good all year round trade, while The Magpie was seasonal, opening from Whit to September: "We

did lunches and teas," recalls Ian McKenzie. "Three courses for 2/6d. Things like roast beef, pie and chicken. But it started to change and got to the stage where people didn't want these kinds of meals at lunchtime, they wanted salads and fish. There were times when we would reach the end of lunchtime and be throwing away up to six dozen Yorkshire puddings. It was very wasteful, so we started an all day menu where people could have anything."

...and that 'anything' was very often fish and chips. People travelled from all over North Yorkshire to feast on Ian McKenzie's fish and chips at The Magpie - they had enjoyed his talent for fish frying from the shop, now they could eat them in the comfort of the café.

Yet he insists that there is no secret for producing perfect fish and chips. It's not rocket science - just a question of getting the batter to right consistency and having the best quality fish. At one time Ian McKenzie would go down to the quay and select his own fish straight from the boats, but when the whole operation was licensed he had to go through the wholesaler.

The business was a real family affair with daughter Alison being 'roped in' from an early age. By the time she was 12 she could turn her hand to anything from washing pots to buttering bread and making up the salads.

She was later to become the 'dessert queen' with her kiwi trifle with almonds and ratafia biscuits a particular favourite with customers.

Even though her parents no longer own the business Alison is still a cornerstone of The

Magpie, and remains its joint owner.

The other half of the partnership, Ian Robson, went to work for the McKenzies in 1980 and gradually took over the business. He bought the property in 2000 and last year completed an ambitious expansion plan which saw a massive £600k investment to support The Magpie's burgeoning reputation.

Originally there were 90 covers in the two restaurant rooms. The Magpie took over the wet fish shop and house next door and converted it to give extra seating, a disabled lift with access from the street, and a bar.

Now The Magpie can accommodate 130 people, which should go a little way to easing the queues which routinely form outside the famous café. These queues have been the source of some publicity in the past; even in January there can be a small gaggle of people waiting to be seated. And at the height of the summer customers are prepared to queue for maybe an hour just to enjoy something off The Magpie menu.

And with the expansion came more jobs - an extra 20 full and part time chefs, waiters and cleaners.

The joy of the place is its family friendliness. The clientele - from toddlers to grandparents - are all welcomed with the same kindness and enthusiasm. And the family friendly ethos extends to the staff too with several generations and a number of siblings working there.

The Magpie has worked hard to gain its reputation as the best fish restaurant in the north of England and the staff work even harder to keep it.

Our hometown

The Magpie Café is but one good reason to visit Whitby. Join us on a whistle-stop tour as we set out to find out what made this little town on the North Yorkshire coast famous the world over.

Whitby

The windswept cliff-tops and natural harbour of Whitby have held a fascination for visitors since long before the haunting silhouette of its famous abbey appeared.
 Romans, Anglo-Saxons and Vikings were all drawn to the spot, sheltering between rugged cliffs at the estuary of the River Esk. Celts founded a monastery there, overlooking the North Sea, and below it a community grew up, relying on the sea for a living.
 Evidence of those origins remain, contributing to the charm which makes Whitby a honeypot for tourists. The imposing ruins of the 13th century abbey dominate the landscape for miles around and the narrow cobbled streets and picturesque cottages of the old town still huddle around the harbour below.
 Within it, the Magpie Café is a draw for visitors in its own right, but Whitby has many other attractions too...

Captain Cook

High on West Cliff stands a statue of Whitby's most famous adopted son. Young James Cook (pictured right) came to the town in 1746 as apprentice to ship owner John Walker. Twenty years later he chose a Whitby-built ship, the Endeavour, for his first voyage of discovery.
 Originally named the Earl of Pembroke, the vessel was a flat-bottomed 'coal and timber' - or cat - craft designed for the coastal trade. It was capacious, able to withstand being run aground and could be managed by a small crew if necessary. Cook's later ships, the Resolution, Adventure and Discovery, were also built in Whitby.
 He set off on that first voyage in 1768, carrying members of the Royal Society to observe the transit of Venus across the sun. They reached Tahiti almost a year later, spent six months charting New Zealand, claimed possession of

Whitby Harbour

eastern Australia, then returned home via New Guinea, Java and the Cape of Good Hope, recording thousands of previously unknown species of plants, fish, birds and animals.

Cook went on to make two further voyages of discovery, becoming the first captain to save his crew from scurvy by carrying large quantities of fresh fruit and vegetables on board.

He was killed by natives in Hawaii in 1779. But the four-storey house in Grape Lane, Whitby where the apprentice seaman pursued his studies, huddled by the chimney breast for warmth, today stands as a museum and a tribute to one of the nation's greatest explorers.

Whitby Harbour

A millennium of maritime heritage rests between the twin stone piers of Whitby's historic harbour.

Countless ships have found a safe haven in its shelter, guided by two lighthouses built in the mid-19th century. But their predecessors dated back much further, giving the original Roman settlement its name: Streoneshalh, bay of the lighthouse.

Today one of the highlights for visitors is the Bark Endeavour, a 40 percent replica of Captain Cook's ship, built in 2001 by one of the town's oldest shipbuilders and permanently berthed in the harbour. The bark - named for its construction of larch planks on an oak frame - is open for pleasure trips throughout the week.

Whitby is also the winter home of tall ship Grand Turk, replica of an 18th century man o'war, which starred in the TV series Hornblower.

A fishy story

A bove the harbour, the distinctive whalebones arch is a lasting reminder of the town's whaling history. Between 1750 and 1830 more than 2,700 whales were killed and brought back to Whitby.

It was a dangerous job and anxious families would scour the horizon when a ship was due in. If a pair of whale jawbones was attached to the mast, they knew no-one had been lost. The pair which form this landmark were presented to the town by Norway in 1963, though due to deterioration these were replaced with a new pair which were found in Alaska, and kindly donated by Whitby's twin town of Anchorage.

Fishing has always been a mainstay of the local

economy although, in line with other UK ports, the Whitby fishing fleet has been halved over the last decade to conserve stocks.

The town knows how to get the best from its catch - freshly caught fish is served up throughout the day at the Magpie Café while in Henrietta Street kippers are still cured in the time-honoured way at Fortune's smoke house.

Brothers Barry and Derrick Brown smoke North Sea herring over fires of oak and beech shavings that have been burning for more than 120 years.

Whitby Abbey and St Mary's Church

Whitby's best-known landmark stands proudly on the clifftop, an enduring reminder of the town's monastic roots.

Founded by Anglo-Saxon King Oswy in AD 657 and led by St Hilda, it was destroyed by Vikings 200 years later and finally re-established by the Benedictines in the 11th century. The remains of the building we see today are mostly from the 13th century.

A stone-flagged pathway leads from the abbey to the nearby parish church of St Mary, parts of which go back to around 1110.

The church was fitted largely by ships' carpenters, which accounts for its distinctive interior. Notable features include its unusual three-decker pulpit and, behind it, a pew belonging to the land-owning Cholmley family, supported by barleycorn twist columns and accessed from an outside staircase.

The Cholmleys' house, next to the church, is now a visitor centre housing archeological finds, computer-generated images and audio-visual displays which recreate the medieval scene. The Church Stairs - 199 in total, leading down to the town - have been a feature of Whitby for around 700 years. Originally brightly-painted timber, they were rebuilt in stone in 1774 when an extra five steps were added.

The literary connection

The Gothic ruins of Whitby Abbey are synonymous with the story of Dracula.

It was against this backdrop that Abraham

Stoker (pictured below) witnessed a shipwreck which inspired his novel and high up on Whitby's West Cliff, at a spot now marked by the Bram Stoker Memorial Seat, he wrote much of his classic Victorian tale.

Stoker drew on his experiences in Whitby to bring the novel to life. Many of the features can be seen today including East Crescent, the holiday home of heroines Mina and Lucy, the fish market, the harbour bridge, Church Stairs, the long stone jetty flanked by sands and, of course, the Abbey and graveyard.

The town's link with Dracula is celebrated in the Dracula Experience, a walk-through attraction featuring life-size models, actors and artefacts including a cape worn by Christopher Lee in his second Dracula film.

There are also regular walks - In Search of Dracula - led by local historian Harry Collett, which tour landmark sites from the book. And twice a year the entire town is taken over by white-faced, black-clad Goths for a weekend festival which has become a highlight of the cultural calendar, featuring music, dancing and the goth-market Bizarre Bazaar.

Other literary figures connected with the town include Caedmon, the earliest known English poet, who became a monk at Whitby monastery, and Charles Dodgson, better known as Lewis Carroll, who wrote much of Alice in Wonderland sitting on Whitby sands.

Bram Stoker

Regular visitors over the years have also included Tennyson, Dickens, Wilkie Collins and Sir Henry Irving.

The jet set

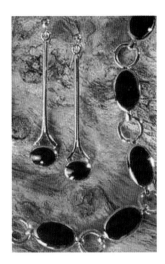

Another of Whitby's claims to fame is jet - the polished black gemstone which adorned every fashion-conscious Victorian woman.

In prehistoric times monkey-puzzle trees (Araucaria) grew abundantly in the area, but over millions of years they were drowned, squashed and fossilised into the hard, light mineral. Jet is found only along a seven-mile stretch of coastline around Whitby.

As long as 6,000 years ago it was used in jewellery, as a talisman to give protection from the evil eye and dreaded leprosy. It came to international attention during the Great Exhibition of 1851 and the red-tiled workshops of Whitby went into overdrive to meet demand for jet jewellery and ornaments. It reached its heyday when Prince Albert died and grief-stricken Queen Victoria wore mourning for the rest of her life.

By 1870 1,500 men, women and children were employed in the industry, but it gradually lost its appeal and the final death knell was sounded by cheaper foreign imports. The sole remaining example of a Victorian jet workshop was discovered during renovation of a derelict property in the town centre. An attic wall was knocked down to reveal a workshop sealed behind it - complete with grinding wheels, high stools and tools. It was carefully dismantled and reassembled at the Whitby Jet Heritage Centre in Church Street.

Famous friends

Few accolades can be more satisfying than to have television's best-known seafood chef tell you he's just enjoyed the best fish and chips he has ever had...

But that's what happened to Ian Robson, and it is one of the rare occasions when the man behind The Magpie Café - known for his modesty and self-effacing nature - allowed himself a grin of pride.

Rick Stein was in Whitby filming for his new television series. He was out on a fishing boat when the skipper Richard Brewer asked where he was going to eat that night. Richard - the man

Rick Stein and Chalky

who first brought scallops to The Magpie kitchen - suggested he try Ian's restaurant.

"To start with he was just another customer," says Ian, "then we recognised him. I remember he had cod and chips and when he'd finished he said it was the best fish and chips he'd ever had."

Indeed he was so impressed that he changed the last programme in his BBC series Rick Stein's

Seafood Lover's Guide, to include The Magpie. It was first broadcast by the BBC in 2000 and showed the cod being fried in beef dripping with lovely chips and mushy peas. In short, Rick described the cod as: "Cod that passeth all understanding". Those comments were to have unexpected consequences. A few weeks after it went out on television the queue of customers wanting to taste The Magpie magic was manic.

But Rick Stein isn't the only personality to have enjoyed the Magpie's hospitality. Ian's predecessor Sheila Mckenzie remembers the time when film director and food writer Michael Winner and actress Jenny Seagrove came to dine: "There was a queue of customers waiting for tables when this young lady came and asked if we realised Michael Winner was outside. It was Jenny Seagrove. We had to be diplomatic, but we managed to get him in early, and he enjoyed his meal. When it came to sweets he said that it was such a good sweet menu, could he possibly have a small portion of each so that he and Miss Seagrove could share?"

Actor Michael York has been to The Magpie too. His secretary telephoned to book a table and the staff made an extra effort to make the table look attractive. But when he arrived he looked so casual that they didn't recognise him and he had to introduce himself.

Chef Brian Turner has cooked in The Magpie kitchen and so has internationally renowned Ken Hom who was doing a demonstration on the

And there are lots of those.

One couple from York loved The Magpie so much that they held their wedding breakfast there 15 years ago with the buzz of holidaymakers helping to make it a special meal. Now they have since introduced their children to the delights of The Magpie and come over from York as often as they can to enjoy the informal and friendly atmosphere.

Another customer willingly makes the hour long drive from Thirsk just to get two regular cod and chips. The reason? "Everything is so clean and unbelievably fresh. In 20 years I don't think I have had a meal which was anything less than delicious…"

"…expect good honest food, prepared freshly from the finest and freshest fish - it's probably only the trawlermen who get fresher fish."

And a couple from Tunbridge Wells in Kent love the Magpie so much that they make the pilgrimage to Whitby twice a year just to eat at The Magpie: "It's well worth the queue, the food is excellent and huge portions."

Then there are the numerous good food awards including 26 years in the Good Food Guide and Egon Ronay's Restaurant of the Year in the Just a Bite Guide.

Sheila McKenzie well remembers the first one which came after one extremely busy Sunday in the late seventies: "A young lady came in and said she'd been out walking with her friends and they'd decided to come in for something to eat. They were very impressed, but we were so busy she didn't dare come and talk to us. And by sheer chance she was from Egon Ronay."

Brian Turner

harbour and used The Magpie for preparation.

Endorsements from personalities like these, together with The Magpie's well-earned reputation, have kept the café in the world's eye - no more so than during the controversy over the queuing which has stumped the local authority and is currently at stalemate.

The thought that a business could be penalised for having too many people queuing caught the imagination of the world's media and broadcasting crews from all over the world descended on Whitby.

"It got huge media coverage," recalls Ian, "I did 20 radio interviews and we had TV channels not just from the UK and Ireland, but from New Zealand, Australia, Singapore and even Russia.

But while worldwide recognition is very welcome, it is the testimonies of ordinary customers who enjoy eating at The Magpie, which are the acid test.

The dark side...

In a town where ghosts are as much a part of the fabric as holidaymakers, it would seem somehow unjust if The Magpie could not boast a live-in spectre of its own.

Fortunately it has at least one - and maybe even three!

Sheila and Ian McKenzie, who ran The Magpie until 1990, are aware of a clerk who used to work in the building when it was Harrowings Shipping Company. Indeed Ian McKenzie has seen him and spoken to him: "I was there painting one day when the café was closed during the winter, and he just walked through the wall. I spoke to him and said something like: 'hello, you here again?' but he didn't reply."

The ghost - always smartly dressed in grey tweeds with a grey flat cap - has appeared on the stairs and in the attic room, where apparently he looks out of the window and across the harbour. He seems to be a kindly figure who brought good fortune: "There was always a lovely homely feel about The Magpie," says Sheila, "and I always believed the two were connected."

One day a visitor came into the café and asked about the ghost, Ian and Sheila described him and the woman produced documents and pictures which suggested it could have been her uncle: "Apparently he used to walk through the town and had a stick with notches on it to show how far he had walked - she said he was a very interesting man."

The ghost of Albert Harrowing - owner of Harrowings Shipping Company and one time occupant of the building - may also have returned to his old haunts, according to Whitby's own spectral specialist Harry Collett.

Harry takes visitors on ghost tours around the town and while he has never actually seen the ghost of Albert Harrowing, he's met a woman who thinks she has: "She told me that he was wearing a Norfolk coat - something in tweed with four or five buttons and breast pockets - and plus fours. Interestingly that's what he might have worn if he had ridden in from his estate at Aislaby. Apparently he was standing in the top right hand corner of the room looking towards the pier."

A customer once asked Ian Robson if he was aware of the spiritual activity in the café. He said that all the time he was eating he was aware of a man beside him who wasn't very happy. He got the feeling that the man resented all the people being in what he considered to be his office. Harry Collett can quite understand that - he says ghosts have a way of making their presence known when they are unhappy with changes.

Indeed one of The Magpie's ghosts appears to have made his presence known on more than one occasion...

Chef Paul Gildroy was locking up one night and tried to go through a door in the restaurant only to find it blocked by a table: "I had been upstairs and there was no other way into the room for anyone to put the table behind the door - that's one of his little tricks."

Then there was the time that a party of 13 had pre-ordered 13 Dover sole. The fish were bought in and prepared and Paul cooked them. He put 13 in the oven...but when he came to get them out there were only 12: "We still don't know what happened to the 13th!

"That was a bit of a disaster - we had to start trimming bits off to make another."

Ian Robson reckons there could be another ghost at The Magpie too, although reports of this jolly old lady have been sketchy: "Apparently she is small and fat and enjoys watching people eating and enjoying their food."

The good news is that the clerk, Albert and the plump, jolly old lady appear to be friendly - and it's only customers with a sixth sense who know they are there.

Whitby Crab starter with Marie rose sauce

INGREDIENTS

2 boiled crabs
(or fresh and still alive to boil
yourself)
Lettuce leaves
(lollo rosso, endive and
little gems)
Lemon to garnish
Marie rose sauce (see extras)

METHOD

If using live crabs, the most humane method is to put the crabs into cold salted water and slowly bring to the boil. Boil for ten minutes, remove from water and chill.

Remove the meat from the cooked crab:
Lay the crab on its back and break off the tail flap. Twist off the claws and legs. Stand the crab on its head, hold firmly and use your thumbs to ease the body out of the shell. Remove the feathery grey gills (known as dead men's fingers) that are attached to either side of the body. Press down on top shell to detach the spongy sac - this is found directly behind the mouth. Cut the honeycomb into four and carefully pick out the white meat with a skewer. Keep the white meat separate from the brown.

Use a teaspoon to scoop out the creamy brown meat from the back shell, then scoop the solid brown meat from inside the flaps. Crack open the claws (using the back of the knife) and remove the meat. Do the same with the legs or you can keep the legs whole for garnish.

To serve, arrange some leaves on a plate and place a spoonful of the brown meat on them, then top with white meat. Finish with crab claws, sliced lemon and brown bread.

"What would the menu of any seafood restaurant be without crab? But at The Magpie it's more than that. Because there's crab, and then there's Whitby crab. The sweet white meat is marvellous, but don't, whatever happens, miss out on the fuller flavoured brown-meat. I well remember as a young boy going on The Scar (between Whitby and Robin Hood's Bay) hunting for Dogger Crabs with Grandad. I'd lift rocks in search of the small crabs - if I'd come face-to-face with a Brown Crab, I reckon I'd have scaled the cliff in my desperation to escape!"

P.G.

Kipper Pate served with Melba Toast

INGREDIENTS

4 large kippers
150g crème fraiche
60g butter (softened)
Juice of 1/2 lemon
Salt and pepper
Slices of thick bread

METHOD

Poach the kippers in a frying pan or deep tray. When cooked, remove from water and chill.

Place crème fraiche, butter, lemon juice and freshly milled black pepper in a food processor. Take the chilled kippers and from the tail remove the central bone from each side of the kipper. This should just lift away from the meat, taking most of the larger bones with it. The meat should then be flaked and the skin removed. Place meat in the food processor and blitz.

Share mixture out between small ramekins, or using two spoons shape into a quenelle (slightly elongated egg shape). Serve with dressed mixed leaves and melba toast.

To prevent the smell of kippers spreading in the house, place the kippers in a jug, totally cover with freshly boiled water and stand for 5 - 6 six minutes, remove from water and serve. Don't bother with wine as kippers are an oily wine destroyer - try Manzanilla Sherry or have a cup of tea.

Whitby is noted for the quality of its kippers, so we couldn't let this opportunity pass without including a recipe made with them. Kipper fillets have already had the larger bones removed, and just need skinning.

I.R.

Magpie seafood taster
(ideal for three to four people to share as a light lunch)

INGREDIENTS

150g mixed cooked crab
(brown and white meat)
150g salmon
150g cooked prawns
150g live mussels
150g live clams
100g smoked salmon
150g each of oak smoked and
cooked salmon (see method)
2 roll mop herrings
100g marinated anchovies
150g live cockles
2-3 king scallops
8 fresh raw crevettes or
langoustines
100g olives
Selection of mixed leaves (lollo
rosso, red chard, little gems and
curly endive)
Marie rose sauce (see extras)

METHOD

Cook the mussels, cockles, clams and crevettes in a
little butter, wine and garlic until the shells open
(discard any that stay shut). Sauté the king scallops
in a little oil for about 30-40 seconds (do not overcook them as they will go tough and chewy). Poach
the salmon in a little water, lemon juice, butter, salt
and pepper. Chill all the seafood well.

Arrange the leaves on a large serving dish and place
the seafood neatly on top. Flake the salmon, slice the
scallops and fan them out. Place the mussels,
cockles, clams and crevettes (all still in their shells)
in and around the other seafood.

Finally do the same with the olives and finish with
endive, slices of lemon and a big pot of sauce.

"When I first came to the Magpie 28 years ago, there would never have
been such a selection of fresh shellfish such as goes into this dish. The
demand wasn't there, and come to that, supplies were hard to come by. It
has to be said now we've never had it so good. This is the perfect lunch
to enjoy with friends. Just open the wine and pick away."

I.R.

Devilled Crab served with Toast

INGREDIENTS

600g crabmeat (equal quantities
of brown and white meat)
150 ml double cream
1 tblsp horseradish
1/2 tsp cayenne pepper
2 sprigs of fresh basil
A small amount of Parmesan
cheese
Fresh breadcrumbs made
from 4 slices bread
Sliced French bread to serve

METHOD

Put the cream into a pan and heat. Add the crabmeat,
horseradish and cayenne, mix with the cream and
heat. When the crab is hot, split between 4 dishes
and sprinkle with breadcrumbs and brown under the
grill. Serve with toasted French bread, a wedge of
lemon and sprig of parsley.

Be careful when seasoning the dish as the crabmeat
will have been boiled in salted water.

Inspired by the connection of Whitby and Dracula, devilled
dishes always tend to be popular, as they give a good 'bite
back'.
Spicy it may be, but the dish still finds a good match in Old
or New World Sauvignon Blanc, or try New Zealand Sauvignon
or Italian Verdicchio, Soave or a top white Rioja.

I. R.

Magpie seafood chowder

INGREDIENTS

600g salmon (skinned, boned
and cut into 4cm squares)
600g white fish (haddock or cod)
skinned, boned and cut into 4cm
squares
12 raw crevettes
8 raw king scallops
500g fresh mussels
400g fresh cockles
500ml fish stock (see extras)
200ml double cream
75g butter
75g plain flour
2 shallots (roughly chopped)
300ml white wine (for poaching)
50g butter
100ml double cream (to finish)
Salt and pepper

METHOD

To make the fish sauce, melt the 75g butter and add the flour to form a paste or a roux. This needs to be cooked until it takes on a sandy texture. Gradually add the fish stock, whisking in a little at a time, bringing back to the boil each time to avoid any lumps. Use all the stock and 200ml of the cream, season and keep warm.

Put the remaining butter and shallots in a separate pan and cook gently. Add the salmon, haddock and white wine. Cover and gently poach for three minutes and then add the shellfish. Poach until the crevettes are pinky orange and the mussels and cockles have opened (discard any which don't open). Add the fish sauce, heat but don't boil and finish with the cream.

"To serve, divide into four bowls, garnish with chopped parsley and serve with lots of crusty bread. Boston eat your heart out!

P.G.

Cullen Skink (Smoked Haddock and Potato Soup)

INGREDIENTS

500g trimmed and skinned
natural smoked haddock
(750g untrimmed)
700g potatoes
(Maris Piper or King Edward)
500g or one large onion
1 clove garlic
2 pints full cream milk
150ml double cream
Knob of butter
Salt and pepper
Parsley (chopped, to serve)

METHOD

Poach the haddock in the milk. Do not boil. When it is just cooked - it should just flake with the slightest pressure - remove and put to one side, retaining the milk.

Peel and roughly chop the potatoes (2 cms dice) and add them to the milk. Peel and roughly chop the onion (2 cms dice), crush the garlic and add both to the milk along with the butter. Return the pan to the heat and cook the potatoes until tender.

Blitz the cooked potatoes, milk, onion and garlic until smooth and add the cream. Place back on the heat and flake the haddock into the soup. Season to taste.

Serve in a soup bowl with chopped parsley and some crusty French stick.

This great Scottish fish soup is a national institution. And we're sure they won't mind we Sassenachs borrowing it so everyone can enjoy. Deserves a decent wine - try Mersault, Californian or New Zealand Chardonnay, Marsanne or Albarino.

I.R.

Magpie Caesar salad

INGREDIENTS

2 cos or 4 little gem lettuce
4 slices white bread
Knob of butter
Freshly-milled black pepper
2 cloves of garlic (crushed)
32 marinated anchovy fillets (8 per portion)
Fresh Parmesan shavings

For the Caesar dressing:

6 tblsp mayonnaise
6 marinated anchovies
1 clove of garlic
2 tblsp grated Parmesan
1 tblsp white wine vinegar
1 tblsp fresh lemon juice

METHOD

First make the dressing. Place the mayonnaise, anchovies, a clove of garlic, grated Parmesan, vinegar, lemon juice and pepper in a food processor and blitz until smooth. Season to taste.
Slice the crusts off the bread and cut into 1cm cubes. Heat a pan with some oil, add the cubed bread and cook until golden. Add the crushed garlic, a knob of butter and some black pepper and cook for a further minute. Place the croutons onto kitchen paper to absorb any excess butter.

Wash the lettuce and divide between four bowls. Add the anchovies, Parmesan shavings and croutons. Drizzling with Caesar dressing and serve.

"If you're not keen on anchovies (or a vegetarian), try using Baco-bits from the supermarket. Left-over dressing can be kept in a jar in the fridge for over a week. It is also good as a dip at parties for chicken goujons or strips of raw vegetables."

P.G.

Tiger prawns in brown ale batter served with smoked paprika mayo

INGREDIENTS

32-40 tiger prawns
(8-10 per portion)
350g plain flour
1 bottle Newcastle brown ale
1 level tsp baking powder
1/2 tsp salt
300g mayonnaise
2 level tsp smoked paprika
(I use hot, but use sweet if you prefer)
2 handfuls of rocket
50ml white wine vinegar
50ml extra virgin olive oil
Salt and pepper
Dripping or oil for deep frying

METHOD

To make the batter, sieve the flour, baking powder and salt into a bowl and make a well in the centre. Pour in the brown ale and whisk into a batter (this should be a smooth consistency, like double cream). Place into the fridge for 20 to 30 minutes before using. Combine the paprika with the mayonnaise.

Heat a deep pan, half full of oil to 175°c, (370f), take the batter and check the consistency - it should be no thicker than double cream. Dip the prawns into the batter, then into the oil and deep fry for four to five minutes until the batter looks golden.

Finish the dish by making a dressing with the olive oil, vinegar and seasoning. Toss the leaves in with the dressing and plate. Top the leaves with prawns and serve with a little pot of the mayo.

Alternatively, use little gem leaves and place 2-3 prawns on each. Ideal for a finger buffet.

"A good match on the widescreen, a cold beer or two in the fridge. A comfortable armchair and a couple of friends visiting. Go on, have a dip!"

I.R.

Sautéed King Scallops and Squid with Butter and Freshly-Milled Black Pepper

INGREDIENTS

12 king scallops
(allow 3 per portion)
200g prepared squid,
cut into strips
100g butter
Black pepper
Garlic mayo (to serve)
Freshly sliced bread (to serve)

METHOD

Heat a sauté pan and add a third of the butter taking care not to let the butter burn. Add the scallops. Depending on size they should only need 30 seconds on each side. Remove from pan and keep warm. Add half the remaining butter and squid and saute in a medium to hot pan - this should need a minute at the most. Add the rest of the butter and the freshly-milled black pepper. Remove from heat so as not to overcook the squid.

Arrange the scallops (three per portion) in the middle of a warm plate and divide the squid between four, over the scallops. Add chopped parsley to the butter and pour over the scallops and squid. Serve immediately with a pot of garlic mayo and a couple of slices of fresh bread.

"Impressive it may sound, but this is a simple no-fuss dish. It also provides an opportunity to enjoy two of the sea's finer products. Scallops and squid are best served lightly cooked so they don't become tough or chewy. Uncork a Chablis, Muscadet, or Pinot Grigio"

I. R.

Magpie Fishcake with minted mushy peas

INGREDIENTS

1.5kg potatoes
(Maris Piper or King Edward)
1.5kg haddock
(skinned and boned)
6 spring onions
Milk to poach
Salt and pepper

Magpie mushy peas (see page 82)
Fresh mint (approx 50g chopped
and add to the peas when ready
to serve)

METHOD

Boil the potatoes in salted water. Poach the haddock in the milk with the spring onions, salt and pepper. When the potatoes are cooked, strain and mash. Strain the haddock and add to the mash, mix gently. Season and chill for 1 hour.

Divide the mixture into eight and shape into cakes. Lightly flour and either pan fry or deep fry in batter.

To serve, put a spoonful of peas onto a plate and place the cake on top, garnish with a sprig of fresh mint and wedge of lemon.

Along with fish and chips, the fishcake is a staple for visitors to Whitby. Your visit is not complete unless you've tried one of the delicious duo. Our version sticks to the traditional principles. Some things, after all, are best left as they are.

I.R.

Grilled salmon with garlic potatoes and green salad

INGREDIENTS

1kg salmon
(skinned and boned)
1.5kg new or baby potatoes
3-4 cloves of garlic
1 romaine lettuce
200g red chard
1 oak leaf lettuce
Splash of oil
Salt and pepper
50g butter

METHOD

Boil the potatoes in salted water until tender, drain and leave to cool slightly. Meanwhile trim the thin white flappy bit of salmon off, as this is quite oily. Cut into four portions, season and grill for about eight to ten minutes. Wash the leaves, and mix together and divide between four bowls, leaving a well in the middle of each. Slice the potatoes (1-1.5cm thick) and heat the oil in a frying pan. Add the potatoes, and season well.

Toss the potatoes frequently to achieve an even colour, crush the garlic and add it to the potatoes (don't burn the garlic as it will taste bitter). Finish the potatoes with the butter and chopped parsley and place them into the middle of the bowls. Place the salmon on top.

"Serve immediately, with a balsamic dressing (simply combine balsamic vinegar, olive oil, a squeeze of lemon juice, salt and pepper. Adjust to taste)."

P.G.

Crab cakes with créme fraiche tartare sauce

INGREDIENTS

1 kg potatoes
(Maris Piper or King Edwards)
500g cooked crabmeat
(brown and white meat mixed)
1 dessertspoon chopped chive
Salt and pepper
Oil for frying

For the crème fraiche tartare:

400g crème fraiche
4-6 gherkins
100g capers in brine
Juice of 1/2 a lime
Salt and pepper

METHOD

Boil the potatoes in salted water. Drain and mash. Add the crab, chives and seasoning, taste and chill.

For the tartare, very finely chop the gherkins and capers, add them to the crème fraiche with the lime juice, season and set aside in the fridge.

Divide the potato and crab mix into eight equal amounts. Roll each into a ball and flatten slightly. Heat the oil in a pan and on a low heat cook the cakes for about four minutes on each side or until golden.

To serve, lightly dress some leaves and place onto plates. Place two cakes onto the leaves and either drizzle the crème fraiche tartare over them or serve in a little dish at the side of the plate. Finish with a wedge of lime.

"Like so many sauces and dressings in this book, tartare can be put into the fridge and kept for three to four days. It can be used as a lighter option to normal tartare sauce with fish and chips."

P.G.

King scallop and goat's cheese bruschetta

INGREDIENTS

8 large king scallops
8 slices French bread
500g goat's cheese
8 cherry tomatoes
4 spring onions
Extra virgin olive oil
Fresh coriander to garnish

METHOD

Toast the slices of bread and drizzle with olive oil. Thinly slice the goat's cheese and place onto the bread. Grill on a medium heat until the cheese starts to melt and brown.

Take the scallops and slice each one into three horizontally. Heat a frying pan with a little oil and sear the scallops - cook for no more than 15 seconds on each side. Remove from the pan so they don't overcook.

Remove the toast and cheese from under the grill. Slice the cherry tomatoes thinly and place onto the cheese. Thinly slice the spring onion into 2 cm strips and place them on the tomatoes. Carefully add three pieces of scallop onto each bruschetta, garnish with fresh coriander, freshly milled black pepper and a drizzle of extra virgin olive oil. Serve immediately.

"Italy meets North Yorkshire - and the resulting marriage is a happy one. These are great for a starter or you could make smaller versions by cutting each slice of bread into three and placing one piece of scallop on each. Great for nibbles with drinks."

P.G.

'Pecten Maximus Scallops are filter-feeding

Mussels and chips with garlic mayo

INGREDIENTS

2kg Maris Piper potatoes
Beef dripping for deep-frying
2kg fresh mussels
75g butter
4 shallots (finely sliced)
2-3 cloves garlic (crushed and roughly chopped)
300ml white wine
200ml double cream
200ml mayonnaise
2 cloves garlic (crushed to a paste)
Parsley (chopped) to garnish

METHOD

Place dripping in a deep pan - no more than half way up - and heat to 150°c (300f). Peel the potatoes and cut length ways 2 to 2 1/2 cm thick. The thicker the chip the better, because they do not absorb as much fat. Blanch the chips (without colour) until firm but soft in the middle. Set aside. Heat the fat to about 175°c ready to finish the chips.

Take the mayonnaise add the garlic paste and some chopped parsley. In a deep pan melt the butter, add the shallots and garlic, lightly fry, turn up the heat and add the mussels and wine, cover with a tightly fitting lid and steam for three or four minutes until all the mussels have opened, discarding any which don't open. Share the mussels between four bowls reserving the cooking liquor, cover to keep warm. Place the pan with the liquor back on the heat and add the cream, bring to the boil and reduce by one third.

Finish the chips by putting them back in the pan of dripping and fry until golden and crispy on the outside, fluffy on the inside. Remove, drain on kitchen paper and lightly salt. The cooking liquor should now have come to the boil and reduced by about a third, add some chopped parsley and share between the four bowls of mussels. Serve immediately with the chips and garlic mayo and a plate full of bread.

There are those who insist only a Belgian beer is the right partner for this dish. Others still go for the traditional Muscadet. For me, a glass of Champagne and this classic dish becomes a perfect lunch.

I.R.

Seafood Risotto

INGREDIENTS

250g risotto rice
1 to 1.5 litres fish stock
1/2 tblsp olive oil
250g fresh salmon
(skinned and boned,
diced to 5cm cubes)
200g cooked prawns
200g fresh mussels
250g fresh cockles
6 – 8 fresh king scallops
(sliced to 1cm thick
medallions)
5 shallots, finely chopped
150ml dry white wine
1 clove garlic, chopped

METHOD

Wash the mussels and remove the beards (the fibrous clump on the side) soak the cockles in cold water to remove any sand from inside.

Put the stock in a pan and heat. Meanwhile in another pan, add the oil and heat. Add the shallots and garlic, reduce the heat and cook until opaque. Raise the temperature to medium heat and add the wine. Poach the salmon - should only take three to four minutes - remove and then add the mussels and cockles. Cook until they open, discarding any which don't. Remove the shellfish and set aside with the salmon. Add the rice to the wine. The rice will absorb the wine quickly, so add some stock a little at a time, stirring frequently to prevent sticking.

Continue to add the stock, a little at a time. The rice begins to change from being very white to slightly opaque with still some whiteness in the middle. Add the salmon, mussels and drained cockles. Continue to add the stock a little at a time, taking care not to break up the salmon when stirring. It should only take about another one to two minutes to cook. The rice should look plump and opaque, be tender and still have a bit of a 'bite'.

Add the prawns and sliced king scallop and adjust the consistency - it should be quite runny. The rice will still absorb the liquid even in the serving dish. Check the seasoning. The heat of the rice should warm through the prawns and cook the scallops

Share the risotto between the dishes and serve with a warm Ciabatta roll. Serve with Vermentino or Gavi di Gavi.

"There are a few different types of risotto rice available - Nano or Aborio are best as they absorb liquid well and hold their shape.
Don't worry if you don't use all the stock or you need extra - rice can absorb at different rates."

P.G.

Pan-fried monkfish with a warm salad of potatoes and Yorkshire blue

INGREDIENTS

4 x 200g fillets of monkfish
(skinned and boned)
400g baby new potatoes
250g Yorkshire blue cheese (or
any other creamy blue cheese)
1 small bunch of spring onions
8 cherry tomatoes
(quartered)
2 handfuls of leaves
(red chard, rocket, radicchio,
lambs leaf and endive)
2 tblsp oil for frying
100ml extra virgin olive oil
50ml white wine vinegar
Juice and zest of 1 lime
Salt and pepper

METHOD

Boil the potatoes in salted water until tender. Drain, quarter and set aside to keep warm. Heat a little oil in a frying pan, add the seasoned monkfish. Turn several times to brown the fish all round, remove and finish cooking in a preheated oven (220°c, gas 8) for three to four minutes. Remove from the oven and rest for two minutes before slicing. Roughly chop the spring onions and crumble the cheese. Toss with the mixed leaves.

For the dressing, mix the extra virgin olive oil with the vinegar, juice and zest of the lime, salt and pepper. Whisk or shake really well to emulsify the dressing.

To serve, add the warm potatoes and cherry tomatoes to the leaves and drizzle with the dressing. Toss the salad to mix the ingredients together. Divide between four bowls. Take the monkfish, and slice each portion into three or four medallions. Place the monkfish on the salad and garnish with a wedge of lime.

" We've never been fans of outlandish flavour combinations at The Magpie. And there's nothing odd about this one. The blue cheese combines surprisingly well with the meaty monkfish. "

P.G.

Poached monkfish with potato risotto and crispy bacon

INGREDIENTS

4 x 200g fillets of monkfish
400ml light fish stock (see extras)
1g saffron stems
1kg new potatoes
2 shallots
1clove garlic
750ml vegetable or chicken stock
175ml double cream
250g garden peas (lightly cooked)
60g parmesan cheese
2 tblsp oil
8 rashers streaky bacon
Salt and pepper
4 sprigs fresh coriander

METHOD

To make the risotto, finely dice the potatoes. Finely chop the shallots and crush the garlic, lightly sauté in the oil, add the potatoes and cook until opaque. Add the vegetable stock, a little at a time until it has been nearly all absorbed and the potatoes are tender. Add the cream and season. Add the peas and parmesan just before serving. Grill or bake the bacon until crispy.

Heat the fish stock, but do not boil. Add the saffron and then the seasoned monkfish. Gently poach for three to four minutes.

Place the risotto into bowls. Slice each piece of monkfish into three, place on top of the risotto. Finish each with two pieces of bacon and a sprig of fresh coriander.

> There was a time when fishermen used to throw the monkfish back. There was yet another when it was used to make mock scampi, so lowly was it regarded. How times change.
>
> I. R.

Grilled skate with black butter

INGREDIENTS

4 x 400g skate wings
200g butter
100g capers in brine (drained)
Juice of 1 lemon
1 tblsp chopped parsley
Butter for brushing the fish
Salt and pepper

METHOD

Skate wing has meat on both sides, but one side is thicker than the other. To help distinguish which side is which, pick up the skate wing and lightly press each side. One side should feel slightly firmer and may be a little pinker.

This is the thinner side and needs to be grilled first, as you always serve the thicker side up.

Under a medium heat grill the thinner side (for about five to six minutes). Brush with butter, season with salt and pepper. Turn the skate over, brush again with butter and season. Grill for about another five to six minutes or until the skate begins to lightly brown. When the fish is cooked, the meat should lift away from the bone easily. Always check this at the thickest part of the fish.

For the black butter, put the butter into a deep pan and heat. It will start to foam and rise up the pan. The butter will change to a hazelnut colour from the centre of the pan. At this stage, gently shake the pan to mix in the darkening butter. When the butter is a nutty brown overall, remove it from the heat and carefully add the lemon juice, making sure it doesn't rise further up the pan and spit. Finally, add the capers and parsley.

Put the skate on a plate and pour over the butter. Serve simply with boiled potatoes and fresh vegetables.

"A classic. What more needs to be said?"

P.G.

Monkfish Skewer with BBQ Sauce

INGREDIENTS

1kg monkfish
(skinned and boned)
8 rashers of dry cure back bacon
4 bananas
8 tomatoes
1 medium onion
(chopped to 2cm dice)
2 celery sticks
(chopped into thin slices)
1 clove of garlic (crushed)
1kg fresh plum tomatoes (or
800g tinned chopped tomatoes)
1 tblsp tomato ketchup
1/2 tsp ground ginger
1/2 tsp cayenne pepper
1/2 tsp Chinese five spice
1tblsp Worcestershire sauce
40g light brown sugar
2tblsp white wine vinegar
Salt and pepper
Knob of butter for brushing
skewers
Oil

METHOD

To make the sauce, heat the oil, add the onion, celery and garlic and cook on a moderate heat to colour lightly. Add the plum tomatoes, ginger, cayenne, Worcestershire sauce, ketchup and a little salt and pepper. Boil the sugar and vinegar together to a light syrup and add to the tomatoes. Cook for about 25-30 minutes or until thickened slightly. Taste and check seasoning.

Pre-heat the grill to a moderate temperature. Cut the monkfish into 12 even pieces (three per portion) peel the bananas, cut in half and wrap each piece with a rasher of bacon. Take a skewer, start with a piece of monkfish, then bacon-wrapped banana, then tomato. Repeat and finish with a piece of monkfish. Season the monkfish and tomato, but not the bacon as this is already salty.

Place under the grill and cook for about 15 minutes, turning once. To serve place the skewer on boiled rice, pour over the juices and put a pot of barbecue sauce on the side. Garnish with lemon and parsley.

"Barbeque sauce can be prepared in advance. The rest is easy. This is a pleasingly adaptable recipe, since any firm-fleshed fish can be used."

P.G.

Pan-fried Monkfish with Caper and Coriander Dressing

INGREDIENTS

400g monkfish (fully trimmed
and skinned) cut into half inch
thick medallions
2 heaped tblsp roughly chopped
coriander
2 heaped tblsp roughly chopped
capers
Juice and zest of two limes
2 cloves garlic, crushed
2 shallots, finely chopped
1 tsp Dijon mustard
4 tblsp olive oil
2 tblsp white wine vinegar
Salt and pepper

METHOD

Heat a frying pan until it just starts to smoke. Add one tblsp oil. Lightly season the medallions of monkfish and carefully place into the pan; cook for one minute on each side over a high heat. Remove the fish from the pan and keep warm.

Add the remaining ingredients to the same pan and bring to the boil, whisking to emulsify the dressing.

Arrange the monkfish on warm plates, and spoon the dressing over the fish. Serve with sprigs of coriander and a wedge of lemon.

Be careful before adding the rest of the ingredients to the pan, remove from the heat to avoid a flare-up when the oil and vinegar are added.

"Monkfish is perhaps my favourite of all fish. It's surprising to think that in the sixties and seventies it was considered worthy only of using as mock scampi. Its meteoric rise to recognition as a prized fish in its own right has naturally been reflected in its price. Try this with a New Zealand Chardonnay, Pinot Noir or Chilean Merlot and you'll agree it's worth every penny."

P.C.

Seared tuna with chargrilled vegetables and red pepper coulis

INGREDIENTS

4 x 200g tuna steaks
For the coulis;
8 red peppers
4 shallots
1 clove garlic
1/2 pt vegetable stock
1/2 tsp Tabasco sauce
2 tblsp balsamic vinegar
2 tblsp dark brown sugar
1 sprig thyme
4 tblsp oil
Salt and pepper

For the Chargrilled Vegetables:

2 red peppers
2 green peppers
2 yellow peppers
3 medium red onions
2 courgettes
1 aubergine
Oil
Salt and pepper

METHOD

To make the coulis, firstly cut and deseed the red peppers. Peel and halve the shallots, peel and crush the garlic. Place all into a roasting tin with the thyme and drizzle with oil. Roast, turning once for about 25 to 30 minutes or until the peppers have lightly charred.

Place into a food processor and blitz with the stock and tabasco. Boil the vinegar and sugar to a syrup and add to the pureed peppers, pass through a sieve and season.

For the vegetables, halve and deseed the red, yellow and green peppers peppers and cut into strips, slice the onion, courgettes and aubergine. Heat a pan over a high heat, add a little oil and add the vegetables a few at a time, shaking until well browned.

Season the tuna, heat a pan, add a little oil and cook over a medium/high heat for two minutes on each side. The tuna should be nicely coloured on the outside and pink on the inside.

Assemble the dish by placing some vegetables in the centre of a plate then pouring coulis carefully around them. Finally, slice the tuna in half at an angle and place on top of the vegetables.

Think pink. So many people still shy away from anything other than tuna cooked the whole way through. This is a shame, because tuna is better by far if seared outside but left pink in the middle.

P.G.

Baked whole sea bass with lemon and chive

INGREDIENTS

4 x 500-550g seabass
(scaled, gutted and trimmed)
3 lemons
250g butter
400ml white wine
Bunch fresh chives
4 shallots
Salt and pepper

METHOD

Take the seabass and, using a really sharp knife, make four or five slits in one side of the fish.Cut two of the lemons in half and into thin slices. Place the lemons into the slits, saving some to go into the stomach cavity with the diced shallots, roughly cut chives and a little butter. Pour over the wine and lightly season. Bake for 12-15 minutes in a hot oven (220°c gas 8).

Put the rest of the butter, juice and zest of the remaining lemon in a pan and gently heat: add the rest of the chopped chives just before serving and pour over the sea bass.

Serve with freshly boiled new potatoes and sautéed vegetables. Good natural ingredients like this need only the lightest touch from the kitchen. Why complicate a good thing?

P.G.

Tuna Niçoise

INGREDIENTS

4 portions fresh tuna
(150-175g per portion)
2 cos or romaine lettuce
150g marinated anchovies
16-20 cherry tomatoes
4 eggs (hard-boiled)
100g fine beans (cooked in
boiling salted water, but kept
crisp to the bite) chilled
200g kalamata olives
300g new or baby potatoes
(boiled and chilled)
Salt and pepper

METHOD

To prepare the salad, wash the lettuce and arrange the leaves into four bowls, slice the egg, halve the tomatoes, half or quarter the potatoes and arrange over the leaves. Do the same with the olives, anchovies and fine beans.

Heat a griddle pan and lightly oil. When the pan starts to smoke add the tuna, cook for one to two minutes each side depending on thickness and taste. Place one piece of tuna on each salad and serve with a balsamic dressing

"My recipe for summer - patio, sunset, glass of good rosé wine. Heaven!"

I.R.

Magpie Fish Pie

INGREDIENTS

1.5 kg potatoes
600g cod (skinned and boned)
400g salmon (skinned and boned)
200g cooked prawns
600ml full cream milk
50g butter
150ml double cream
10-15g fresh tarragon, chopped
10g fresh chives chopped
1 level tblsp corn flour
1 tblsp lemon juice
1 tsp Worcestershire sauce
1 tsp Tabasco sauce
1/2 tsp English mustard
2 tblsp mayonnaise
Salt and pepper
150g mature cheddar (grated)

METHOD

Peel and roughly chop the potatoes, boil in salted water until thoroughly cooked through, drain and mash with half the butter and a drop of the milk.

Lightly poach the cod and salmon in the remainder of the milk and butter and season with salt and pepper. Do not overcook, as the dish will cook further in the oven. Drain the fish and put the milk back on a very low heat. Place the fish into an ovenproof dish and add the prawns.

To make the sauce, mix together the cream, corn flour, tarragon, chive, lemon juice, Worcestershire, tabasco and mustard to a slack paste and add to the hot, but not boiling, milk. With a whisk, stir the sauce until it thickens. Again, do not boil. Remove from the heat, and add the mayonnaise. Check the consistency (too thick add more cream, too thin add more corn flour mixed to a paste with cream). Check the seasoning. Pour over the fish, top with the mashed potato and finish with grated cheddar. Place into a preheated oven (220°c gas 8) for about 20-25 minutes and serve

"A good fish pie takes time to prepare. And a good one is well worth the effort! This one is up there with the best.

I. R.

Brochette of Salmon and King Scallop with Horseradish Dressing

INGREDIENTS

150g salmon, cut into one inch cubes (allow 2 cubes per person)
8 king scallops (allow 2 per skewer)
100ml olive oil
1 clove garlic
Juice of half a lemon
Chopped chives
Salt and pepper
Horseradish dressing (see extras)
Mixed leaves to serve

METHOD

Make a marinade using the oil, lemon juice, garlic and chive. Add the salmon and marinate for 20 minutes. Put two pieces of salmon and two scallops alternately onto a skewer, place on a grilling tray and grill for 3-4 minutes. Turn the skewer and grill for a further 3-4 minutes.

To serve, place some leaves on a plate and drizzle with horseradish dressing. Serve immediately.

"A dish such as this is a good excuse to uncork a fine white Burgundy, Puligny or Chassagne-Montrachet, or Chablis Grand Cru. You'll have time to savour the wine as there's little effort needed to create this dish. Nevertheless the end result is spectacular and tasty – and it's great on the barbecue too."

I. R.

The Chef's Tale...

A knock at the kitchen door and a fisherman bearing a basket full of scallops...it's hard to believe that this could have been the beginning of a new era for The Magpie Café.

But Ian Robson reckons it was.

The fisherman was skipper Richard Brewer, he brought the scallops to Ian and asked if he wanted them. Ian and the then chef Elaine Middlemas turned them into Coquille St Jacques with a simple white sauce and mashed potato and the dish went down so well with the customers that the kitchen began to get more adventurous.

It was the beginning of the nineties and, thanks to the growing number of cookery programmes on the television, customers were beginning to look for something different. They still loved the fish and chips for which The Magpie is world famous, but now their taste buds had been tempted.

Mussels appeared on the menu along with special fish pies and other different fish dishes and The Magpie developed its own signature dish - a special chowder. Although the dish had been mainstay of the southern states of America for decades, The Magpie did its own 'take' on the dish and it proved a winner.

The most exotic fish current chef Paul Gildroy has ever had to prepare was a bright blue and yellow parrot fish: "We don't get them in the local market, but our fish merchant imported some and asked if we'd like to try it. I'd never seen a parrot fish before - it was a bit different and I thought it would be a good experience.

"We oven baked it with the skin on - and I have to say it looked better than it tasted. It was OK, but it was quite bland really and I don't think we'll be rushing to put it back on the menu."

Whitby born and bred, Paul got his professional qualifications at Yorkshire Coast College, but before that he worked at The Magpie from the age of about 12 buttering bread and rumbling potatoes.

He gained much of his practical experience from the boss, Ian Robson, who in turn had been schooled by his predecessor Ian McKenzie. Ian Robson had a distinct advantage - his father and grandmother were both chefs and his

Paul Gildroy (left) and Ian Robson

▶

maternal grandparents ran a fish and chip shop - so catering really was in his blood.

Originally he was going to be a painter and decorator, but after three years of trying found out he was allergic to the paint, so he went to work in the plastics industry.

Then he met Alison McKenzie, daughter of then owners Ian and Sheila McKenzie and he found himself helping out at The Magpie plating up bread and butter and traditional three-course meals and mashing huge pans of potatoes.

In those days there were just five varieties of fish - cod, haddock, plaice, lemon sole and halibut. The fish monger would go to the market every morning and they would use what was easily obtainable.

Gradually Ian Robson learned the trade and as the McKenzies eased into retirement, he and Alison took over the business in 1990.

He and Paul Gildroy have shared the cooking with Paul learning many of his practical skills from Ian. He loves the fact that The Magpie menu is extensive and challenging: "We have ten or 12 different varieties of fish every day and like to try and do something different. We try to captivate the clientele by keeping up with the trends.

"At one time it was all fried fish, but tastes have changed. We aim for healthy eating and we have a 'Watcher of Weight' menu with grilled and poached fish using olive oil and low fat ingredients."

Paul knows that the most important thing about cooking is the quality of the ingredients: "If you start with the best ingredients, you are half way there. We have a very good relationship with Dennis Crooks our fishmonger and he knows the quality we want. Price is never an issue because quality comes before everything.

"And over the years customers have come to know the difference in quality and to appreciate it more. We buy big flaky fillets of cod and when someone has enjoyed that they realise it is a tremendous experience compared with anything else they have ever eaten."

Paul's recipes evolve; some he has developed himself, some are things he has eaten elsewhere and given his own twist and others he gets out of books and adapts to The Magpie standard. But everything is prepared with the satisfaction of the customers as the number one priority: "They pay our wages and our job is to make sure they are happy and come back again."

What's Paul's favourite? "I have lots of favourites because I love fish, but I suppose it has got to be monkfish. I like it pan fried or roasted and served with a few leaves and a dressing and hazelnut butter. Just four ingredients, but they go together so well.

"I like simplicity - the majority of recipes I use are very simple. I don't use too many ingredients because they overpower the flavour of the fish. Fish is very delicate and you need to treat it with respect."

The Magpie Café builds its menus around the outstanding fresh seafood available on its doorstep.

Customers can enjoy the distinctively-flavoured Whitby crab, kippers and haddock – all from local suppliers or straight from the fish market opposite the restaurant.

Traditional fish and chips with mushy peas and tartare sauce

INGREDIENTS

4 fillets of fresh cod or haddock (about 180g per fillet or 200g for haddock to allow for the skin)
2kg Maris Piper potatoes
Beef dripping for frying

For the batter:

500g plain flour
200g self-raising flour
1/2 tsp baking powder
Approx 1lt chilled water (you may need more or less as flours can absorb differently)

* Mushy peas and tartare sauce; see p81/extras

METHOD

Make the batter by sieving the flour into a bowl, add the baking powder then gradually add the water whisking continuously to avoid any lumps. The batter should be the consistency of single cream (too thick and the batter will be crisp on the outside yet stodgy on the inside). Place in the fridge to chill.

Slowly heat the dripping to approx 150°c (300f) in a large pan (the dripping should only come no more than half way up the pan, any more and you run the risk of overflowing).

Peel potatoes and cut into thick chips (the thicker the better as thicker chips absorb less fat) rinse and pat dry. Carefully add the chips to the fat and cook until soft but still slightly firm, remove and cool slightly.

Turn up the heat and heat to 175°c (370f). Take the fillets of fish one at a time, dip them into the batter and gently lay them into the dripping. These should take about seven to eight minutes to cook and the batter should look light, golden and crispy. Remove and place onto kitchen paper to drain. Place the chips into the hot fat and cook until crisp and golden, again place onto kitchen paper to drain.

To serve, warm four plates put a piece of fish on each. Share the chips between the plates. Put a spoonful of mushy peas on each and a big dish of tartare sauce and a wedge of lemon.

The great British dish whether it be wrapped in yesterday's newspaper or served piping hot on a plate. However you enjoy it, this is the dish that made The Magpie famous. Here's how we prepare our version of the classic.

I.R.

Mushy Peas

INGREDIENTS

400g dried marrowfat peas
1 tsp bicarbonate of soda
1 level tsp salt
1 level tsp sugar
1/2 tsp pea green colouring

Optional:

50g chopped, fresh mint leaves

METHOD

Wash peas in water, drain and repeat twice. Cover the peas with water so it is three times the depth of the peas. Leave to soak overnight.

Rinse and drain the peas twice, then cover with water. Add the salt, sugar and pea green. Bring to the boil (skim if necessary), reduce the heat to a simmer for 45 minutes to 1 hour, until the peas lose their shape and are soft.

Add the mint if required.

We felt the marvellous mushy pea deserved a page all to itself, such is its importance as an accompaniment to that king of dishes, fish and chips

P.G.

Magpie trio

INGREDIENTS

600g salmon
400g lemon sole
(skinned weight, preferably
in four fillets)
12 king scallops
150g butter, chilled
100ml lemon juice
1/2 litre fish stock
Chives
Salt and pepper
Oil

METHOD

Ask the fishmonger to skin and bone both the salmon and sole. Portion the salmon into four pieces. Fold the sole fillets in half, making sure that the side that had the skin on is on the inside.
Heat the fish stock and poach the salmon and sole in it (this will take about 3 to 4 minutes). Remove from the pan and keep warm. Pour half the liqour and all of the lemon juice into another pan and reduce by half.

Meanwhile heat a sauté pan, add a little oil and sear the scallops, turning once (do not cook for more than thirty seconds on each side). Remove from the pan and keep warm.

Add the chilled butter a little at a time to the reduced stock and lemon, whisking it in. Once all the butter has been added, remove from the heat. Do not boil.

On 4 plates, arrange a piece of salmon, a piece of sole and 3 scallops. Add some chopped chives to the lemon butter and drizzle over the fish and scallops. Serve with fine beans and potatoes or salad.

I had a dish similar to this in Portugal a few years back.
The menu simply said 'trio of market fish, grilled'.
The fish tasted like it had been caught that morning -
which it probably had. This is The Magpie's own version.
Perhaps not very surprisingly, it's one of the most popular
dishes on our menu.

P.G.

Salmon en croute with crisp green salad

INGREDIENTS

1 x 600g fillet of salmon
(skinned and boned)
150g shallots
1 tblsp light brown sugar
100ml vegetable stock
250g fresh spinach
6 cherry tomatoes
2 sprigs fresh thyme
500g fresh puff pastry
100g butter
1 egg
Salt and pepper

METHOD

Peel and roughly slice the shallots, heat half of the butter, add the shallots and cook until they start to go golden. Add the sugar, let it dissolve to form a syrup and add a little stock, bring to the boil and reduce to a syrup. Continue this process until you use all the stock and add some ground black pepper. Leave to cool slightly.

Wilt the spinach in a pan with a little butter, season and drain off any excess liquid. Cut the tomatoes in half and pick the thyme into small sprigs, discarding the main stalk.

Take 250g of the puff pastry and roll it into a rectangular shape (slightly larger than the piece of salmon). This is the base of the *en croute*. To stop the base from rising during cooking, make small holes in the pastry. Place the piece of salmon onto the pastry and season with salt and pepper. Place the tomatoes on the salmon, then the spinach, followed by the shallots and finally the thyme. Take the rest of the pastry roll out again to a rectangle. Run a lattice cutter over the pastry and gently open it up. Dab a little water on the base and place the latticed pastry over the top, press lightly to bond together, whisk the egg and, with a brush, put the egg onto the lattice. Trim the edges to look neat and place into a preheated oven (180ºc gas 6) for about 25-30 minutes or until the pastry is puffed up and golden.

Remove from the oven and rest for a couple of minutes before slicing into four and serving with a crisp dressed green salad.

When I think of dishes I try and put my own little twist into them. Here I have introduced sweet caramelised shallots, which marries well with the salmon and cuts through its natural oiliness.

P.G.

Cod in paper parcel with olives, cherry tomatoes, garlic and spinach

INGREDIENTS

4x 250g cod fillets (skinless)
16 kalamata olives (pitted)
12 cherry tomatoes (cut in half)
4 cloves of garlic (thinly sliced)
500g fresh spinach
100g butter
Salt and pepper
4 sheets baking parchment
(approx 30cm x 30cm)

METHOD

Lay the parchment flat and place a piece of cod on each. Season and cover each with spinach. Divide the olives, tomatoes and garlic between the four and finish with butter and a little more seasoning. Wrap them so they look like a Christmas cracker, place into a preheated oven (225°c gas 8) for eight to nine minutes.

The parcel should look puffed and the liquid inside bubbling.

Serve immediately with a salad of leaves tossed with vinaigrette.

This is worth it for the aroma alone. When the parcels are opened, memories of warm Mediterranean nights will come flooding back.

I.R.

Cod wrapped in Parma ham with pan haggerty

INGREDIENTS

4 x 200g fillets of cod
(skinned and boned)
12 slices of Parma ham
2kg potatoes
(Maris Piper or King Edward)
1 large onion
300g mature English cheddar
2 good sprigs of thyme
600ml chicken or
vegetable stock
50g butter
Salt and pepper
4tblsp oil

METHOD

Peel and thinly slice the potatoes and stand in cold water to avoid discolouring. Peel and thinly slice the onion, remove the thyme from the stalks and grate the cheddar. Butter an ovenproof dish (approx 25cm square) and layer the potato, onion, thyme and cheese, reserving 100g of cheese for the top. Season each layer with pepper only as the stock and cheese will have enough salt in. There should be at least three layers. Pour over the stock to just under the top layer. Grease one side of a sheet of foil and cover the potatoes. Bake (on 200°c gas 7) for about 45mins. Remove from the oven, take off the foil - the potatoes should be tender - and sprinkle the remainder of the cheese on top. Return to the oven for another 20 minutes or until golden.

Season the cod and wrap each fillet with three slices of Parma ham making sure that the ends of the ham are tucked under the fish. Secure with a couple of cocktail sticks. Heat the oil in a pan and place them in topside down to seal them. Turn after a minute. After a further minute put the fillets into the oven - turned up to 220°c gas 8 - and bake for about eight minutes. Remove the cod from the oven and allow to rest for two minutes before slicing each fillet into three pieces.

To serve, place a good spoonful of the potatoes onto four plates, fan out the fish and set it next to the potato. Serve with a selection of buttered vegetables.

"Parma ham and cod are by now an established partnership. Here we add an element from northern traditional cooking to provide a fitting accompaniment."

P.G.

Cod with an anchovy crust served with dauphinois potatoes

INGREDIENTS

4 x 250g fillets of cod (skinned and boned)
10 slices of white bread
150g marinated anchovies
1 clove garlic
Juice of 1/2 lemon
30g butter
Fresh parsley (chopped)
Salt and pepper

For the potatoes

1.5kg King Edward potatoes
150ml milk
150ml double cream
2 cloves garlic (crushed)
200g mature cheddar
Butter for greasing dish
Salt and pepper

METHOD

Peel and thinly slice the potatoes. Heat the milk and cream with the crushed garlic, salt and pepper. Lightly butter an ovenproof dish and layer the potatoes, pour in the cream and cover with foil, bake for 40 minutes (200°c gas 7). After 40 minutes remove the foil, cover with the cheese, and return to the oven for another 20-25 minutes.

For the crust, blitz the bread and add the anchovies, garlic, lemon juice, parsley, pepper, and 30g soft butter until evenly mixed.

Take the fillets of cod, lightly season, and cover with the breadcrumbs. Bake for 12-15 minutes (200°c gas 7) or until the crust is golden.

Call them dauphinois potatoes if you prefer - but to us northern lads they're stovies. Whatever name you choose, this is a hearty, satisfying meal and the anchovy crust adds some 'bite' to the dish.

P.G.

Baked cod with tomato and herb salad

INGREDIENTS

4 x 250g fillets cod
(boned and skin left on)
400g ripe red tomatoes
200g yellow tomatoes
100g cherry tomatoes
4 shallots, finely sliced
1 dessert spoon chopped parsley
1 dessert spoon chopped coriander
1 dessertspoon chopped chive
1 dessertspoon chopped basil
60ml white wine vinegar
75ml extra virgin olive oil
Salt and pepper
Oil for frying

METHOD

To prepare the salad, cut the red and yellow tomatoes into six or eight depending on size. Cut the cherry tomatoes in half, and then mix them all along with the herbs and shallots. Make a dressing using the oil, vinegar and seasoning but don't pour over the tomatoes until you are about to serve the salad.

Lightly season the cod and heat an ovenproof pan with a little oil. Gently place the cod, skin side down, cook for about two minutes. Turn the fish over, cook for a further minute then put into a preheated oven (220°c, gas 8) for six to eight minutes.

When you are ready to serve, add the dressing to the tomatoes, lightly toss to mix and put onto plates. Place the cod on top of tomatoes, skin side up and serve with a dish of sautéed potatoes.

If you want to create a sensation at your next soirée, transform the salad into superb bruschetta topping by adding four crushed cloves of garlic and another two tablespoons of olive oil. Serve on freshly toasted bread. These are one to be served with sunglasses balanced on forehead, in true Italian style.

I. R.

Whole Dover sole with brown shrimp butter and a warm salad of new potatoes and fine beans

INGREDIENTS

4x whole Dover soles (gutted
and skinned)
100g brown shrimp (peeled)
150g butter
2 shallots finely chopped
30g chopped parsley
Salt and pepper

Salad:

400g new potatoes
250g fine beans
4 shallots finely sliced
50ml white wine vinegar
50ml extra virgin olive oil
Salt and pepper

METHOD

Boil the potatoes, and while they are cooking grill the Dover sole under a medium heat (the eyes should be facing up, this is the thickest side and the side on which it will be served)

To prepare the shrimp butter, heat the butter in a pan, roughly chop the shrimp and add it to the butter, also add the finely chopped shallots and lightly cook - the shrimp will go tough if over cooked - and finish with the chopped parsley, keep warm.

When the potatoes are nearly cooked, add the fine beans and cook until tender, (about one and a half to two minutes), then drain well. Add the oil, vinegar, salt, pepper and shallots, toss and keep warm.

To serve, place the Dover sole onto the plate, spoon over the shrimp butter and serve with the warm salad of dressed new potatoes and fine beans.

Looks good? Yes. Tastes even better. As British as can be, and a match for anything the world over.

P.G.

Turbot fillet with tartare veloute

INGREDIENTS

4x 300g fillets of turbot
500ml fish stock (see extras)
200ml double cream
75g capers (drained and squeezed)
75g gherkins
50g anchovies (marinated are best)
30g chopped parsley
2 shallots (finely sliced)
Champ and seasonal vegetables to serve

METHOD

Heat the fish stock in a pan with the shallots and gently poach the turbot. Remove from the pan and keep warm. Reduce the fish stock by half, finely chop the gherkins, capers and anchovies and add them to the stock with the cream. Reduce by a further third so that the sauce is the thickness of double cream.

To serve, pipe some champ onto the plates and place the turbot fillets slightly to the side. The sauce should partly cover the fish. Serve with seasonal vegetables.

We experiment with sauces all the time in the kitchen - if they pass our chef's taste test, they might find a place on the menu. But this is one we find hard to beat. The flavours are perfect with delicious white fish.

P.G.

Roast haddock with caramelised shallot and garlic with champ

INGREDIENTS

4 x 200g fillets of haddock
(skin on and boned)
500g shallots
8 tblsp oil
1 bulb of garlic
4 tblsp light brown sugar
150g butter
300ml vegetable stock
1.5 kg potatoes
6 spring onions
100ml double cream
Salt and pepper

METHOD

Peel the shallots - if large, cut in half. Peel the garlic. Heat three tablespoons of oil and fry the shallots and garlic giving them plenty of colour - this adds to the flavour. Add the sugar and half of the butter. Lower the heat to allow the butter and sugar to melt and combine to form a syrup. Bring to the boil and add the stock a little at a time, keeping the liquid syrupy. When all the stock has been added the garlic and shallots should look glazed and the liquid syrupy. Add some freshly ground pepper.

Preheat the oven to 220°c (gas 8).

For the champ, boil the potatoes in salted water, drain and mash with the rest of the butter and cream. Season to taste and add the chopped spring onions. Keep warm.

Season the haddock and heat the remainder of the oil in a pan suitable to go into the oven. Place the haddock fillets skin side down into the pan and cook on a high heat to crisp the skin (for about a minute). Turn the fish over and cook for a further minute. Put the pan into the oven and bake for about six minutes.

To serve, put a good spoonful of champ onto each plate, place the haddock onto the champ and spoon the shallot and garlic around, reserving some of the syrup to drizzle over the fish. Serve with a dish of seasonal vegetables. A perfect alternative to the Sunday roast!

P.G.

Plaice with puy lentils and bubble and squeak cake

INGREDIENTS

4x 300g fillets of plaice
(trimmed and boned)
400g puy lentils
1 medium carrot
(very finely chopped)
1/2 a medium onion
(very finely chopped)
1/2 stick of celery (very finely
chopped)
4 new potatoes
(about 125g, very finely
chopped)
200ml vegetable stock
50g butter

For the Bubble and Squeak Cake

1.5 kg potatoes
1/2 Savoy cabbage
(finely sliced)
1 medium onion
(finely sliced)
Salt and pepper
50g butter
Oil to sauté

METHOD

Boil the potatoes in salted water. Drain and mash. Sauté the finely sliced onion and cabbage for a couple of minutes, retaining the crispness, and season.

Combine the mash, onion and cabbage together and chill slightly.

In a pan cook the lentils, finely chopped onion, celery, carrot and potato with the stock until the lentils have absorbed most of the liquid and the vegetables are tender - about 25-30 minutes.
While the lentils are cooking, take the mash mix and divide into four. Mould each one into a shape like a wheel. Lightly butter each and place into a preheated oven (gas 8, 220°c) for about 15-18 minutes, turning once. They should be golden brown on each side.

Either pan-fry or grill the plaice - pan-frying is preferable because it gives the fish more colour and flavour. Preheat a pan. Add a little oil, lightly season the fish and place flesh down, cook for about three to four minutes and turn the fish over cooking for a further three to four minutes.

To present the dish, take the hot lentils and stir in 50g butter - this enriches the lentils. Place a spoonful on each plate, put the plaice partly on them and place the bubble and squeak cake at the side. Garnish with a wedge of lemon and sprig of parsley.

Enjoy this dish - but make sure you do so at its best. Plaice is at its best during the winter months. Unless you can't wait to give this recipe a go, avoid it from May until mid-August.

P.G.

Lemon sole stuffed with crab and spring onion served with mussel beurre blanc-crushed new potatoes

INGREDIENTS

4 x 150g fillets of lemon sole
(skinned and boned)
400g crab meat
(brown and white meat mixed)
4 spring onions
500g fresh mussels
200ml white wine
3 shallots (finely sliced)
200ml double cream
150g butter
Small bunch fresh chives
800g new potatoes
50ml extra virgin olive oil
Salt and pepper

METHOD

Take one fillet of sole at a time and place flat in a freezer bag. Use the side of a large knife to flatten the fish so that it is an even thickness. Very lightly season the skin side, combine the crab and spring onion and divide the mixture between the four fillets. Spread over the sole. Starting at the tail end of the fish - which will probably be the thinnest end - roll the whole thing up, put a cocktail stick through the flappy piece and place the fish on that side. Season and lightly butter.

Place on a baking tray and bake in a hot oven (220°c gas 8) for about eight minutes. The fish should feel firm if lightly pressed.

For the mussel beurre blanc, place the wine and shallots into a pan and bring to the boil. Add the mussels and cover with a tightly closing lid. Steam until they open, remove and keep to one side. Next add the cream, bring back to the boil and reduce by about half, reduce the heat and add the butter a little at a time, shaking the pan to mix in the butter (do not boil, as the sauce may separate). Return the mussels to the pan to warm through and add some chopped chives. To make the crushed potatoes, simply boil in salted water, drain and with a fork lightly crush the potatoes.

To serve, use large bowls, put a spoonful of potatoes in the centre, drizzle lightly with oil. Slice the sole in half diagonally and place the fish on the potatoes. Divide the mussels between the four, placing them around the potatoes and sole, and pour the sauce over them. Finish with a wedge of lemon and a couple of chives crossed over each other.

Fillet of sea bass with Pernod sauce and celeriac crisps

INGREDIENTS

4 fillets of sea bass
(scaled and boned)
250g butter
100ml Pernod
1 celeriac
Fresh coriander to garnish
Oil for pan-frying

METHOD

Peel the celeriac and cut into four. Using a potato peeler, peel the celeriac into thin strips. Deep-fry until golden.

Cut each fillet of sea bass into two and lightly season. Put the Pernod into a pan, bring to the boil and reduce by half. Gradually whisk in the butter but do not boil as the sauce will separate. Set aside and keep warm. Heat the oil in a frying pan and add the sea bass. Cook on quite a high heat for about a minute on each side.

To serve, place some sauce onto a plate, the two halves of sea bass fillet on top of each other and finish with celeriac crisps and coriander to garnish.

"If the sauce separates, add a drop of boiling water and whisk in. Should salvage the situation."

P.G.

Pan-fried halibut with wild mushroom and Tarragon cream

INGREDIENTS

1.5kg halibut (filleted)
500g fresh wild mushrooms
(the dried variety will need
soaking in water for an hour or
so before use)
400ml double cream
15g fresh tarragon
75g butter
Oil
Salt and pepper

METHOD

Cut the halibut into six steaks and lightly season.
Heat half the butter in a pan. Add the mushrooms
and sauté lightly, add the cream and reduce by a
third. Meanwhile, heat a little oil in a frying pan and
add the halibut flesh side down. Cook on a medium
heat for about three minutes or until golden.
Turn once and cook again for three to four minutes.

The cream should have reduced. Turn down the heat
and add the rest of the butter. Shake the pan to mix,
add the fresh tarragon leaves. Do not boil the cream
as it may separate.

Just before serving place some boiled rice onto the
plate, put the halibut partly over it and pour the sauce
over both the halibut and plate. Garnish with a sprig
of fresh tarragon.

The meatiest of fish - enjoyed at its best here
with a silky creamy sauce.

P.G.

Poached brill with Provençal style vegetables

INGREDIENTS

4 x 200g fillets of brill
500ml light fish stock
(see extras)
500g fresh ripe tomatoes
(plum tomatoes have a good
intense flavour)
2 cloves garlic
1 large aubergine
2 courgettes
1 large onion
1 head of broccoli
100g fine beans
2 tblsp chopped parsley
Salt and pepper
6 tblsp oil

METHOD

Cut the courgettes into slices about 1cm thick, place on a tray and lightly cover with salt and then cling film. Cover for about an hour to draw out some of the moisture and bitterness. Roughly chop the aubergine and onion. Cut the fine beans in half and broccoli into small florets. Cut the tomatoes into quarters and squeeze them to remove most of the seeds; roughly chop the remaining flesh.

Heat the oil in a pan and lightly cook the onions and crushed garlic. Add the tomatoes and a little salt and pepper, bring to the boil and simmer for 15 to 20 minutes until some of the liquid has evaporated. Rinse the courgettes and add to the tomatoes with the aubergines. Cook for a further five minutes. Add the broccoli and fine beans, cook for two minutes more and adjust for seasoning. Finish with the parsley.

Poach the lightly-seasoned brill in the fish stock - this should take only five or six minutes.

To serve, place the vegetables onto a plate and place the brill, so it overlaps slightly, onto the vegetables. Garnish with a sprig of parsley.

Brill is a little harder to find than other fish but place an advance order with your fishmonger and you will be well rewarded.

P.G.

The

isherman's Tale

The Magpie and fisherman Bob Marsden is a match made - maybe not in Heaven - but certainly in Whitby. For Bob is a master at catching salmon and The Magpie chefs have the skill to cook it to perfection.

"They really have the expertise with salmon," says Bob. "And it's the same with the fish and chips - perfect and never soggy."

It is praise indeed from the man who has spent more than 50 years fishing the waters of the North Sea - and, just lately, swimming in them: "I've had one or two dips recently and I've ▶

decided swimming around in the sea in the dark at 72 is not a good idea."

But in his long career Bob Marsden has learned respect for the sea and for Mother Nature and to rely on his expert seamanship to get him safely back into harbour.

Born into a fishing community, Bob found himself thrust into the industry at the age of 12 after his father - a deep sea fisherman - had been killed in an accident in the North Atlantic. Bob was given special permission to leave school and begin earning to help support the family.

He started picking winkles inshore on the North Sea, learned how to open mussels 'to give to the big guys to go out fishing' and graduated to catching the wild salmon.

In his heyday he supplied The Magpie with as much wild salmon as the café needed: "And I could guarantee that they didn't need to refrigerate it because it had only been caught an hour or so before."

Today he still goes salmon fishing, but, for safety's sake, he tends to stick to stick to the three miles north to north west of Whitby: "The licence allows us to fish 17 nautical miles, but the boats are getting older and so are the occupants."

But he prides himself on the fact that if The Magpie wants a 20lb salmon he can still provide it.

Fishing has become much more restricted in recent years; where they used to go out six days a week now they can only go Monday to Friday. The £715 fee the fishermen pay to the Environment Agency allows them to fish from April 1st to the last day of August, although no salmon can be caught until June 1st - and there are hefty fines if one manages to slip through the net.

"You can keep your trout and your sea bass and everything, but it's a £5,000 fine if you catch a wild salmon before June 1st."

Bob reckons Mother Nature has given salmon a sixth sense which gives them a fighting chance against the fishermen: "If a salmon touches a net then you can say goodbye to that fish because it will never be caught. Mother Nature has taught it the difference between a net and a rock and it will never get caught in a net."

He also has great respect for the seals which live in the North Sea - even though as competitors for the catch, they are a nuisance: "I never saw a seal here until 1947, but when the naval demolition was going on they moved down here from the Farne Islands where they lived. We've got more seals on the Yorkshire coast than any other coast in England."

But while Bob accepts that the seals have a right to live in the North Sea, he knows that if they mark a fish, its value in the fish market drops from around £4 a pound to £1.50 - which is when Bob steps in and takes it home for his supper.

"You know that seals don't touch anything only healthy fish so if a salmon has been marked by a seal you know it's OK."

Farmed salmon? Well that's another story: "The taste of wild salmon compared with farmed salmon is like chalk and cheese - they are nothing like each other and people know that. I've heard that people will ring up and ask if it's wild salmon and if it's not they pick something else off the menu.

"Trouble is that farmed salmon only lives in one place. Wild salmon live fast lives and can clean themselves jumping out of the water to get rid of the waste and the parasites. Farmed salmon can't do that."

So, like The Magpie, in Bob's own kitchen at home it's nothing but wild salmon - caught by the master.

Rhubarb crumble

INGREDIENTS

Rhubarb:

2kg rhubarb
200g caster sugar

Crumble topping:

200g soft butter
200g oats
200g Demerara sugar
200g plain flour

METHOD

Prepare the rhubarb by washing and chopping into 2 to 3cm lengths. Very lightly poach with the sugar. Drain off any excess liquid.

To make the crumble topping, place all ingredients in a bowl and rub together until evenly mixed. Place on a baking tray and bake at 180°C until golden (approximately half an hour). Stir the mixture a few times during baking.

Remove from oven and place onto cooked rhubarb. Return to oven for a further five minutes. Serve with custard, cream or ice cream.

Easy, tasty and comfortingly familiar. I never remember it tasting this good back in schooldays.

P.G.

Magpie sticky toffee pudding

INGREDIENTS

Pudding:

150g dried dates
300ml boiling water
1 tsp bicarbonate of soda
165g golden caster sugar
65g butter
2 eggs, beaten
225g plain flour
1 tsp baking powder
2 tsp vanilla essence

Toffee sauce:

265g dark brown sugar
135g butter
1 cup of double cream

METHOD

For the pudding, put the dates and bicarbonate of soda in a bowl and cover with boiling water.

In a separate bowl, mix together the butter and sugar, and then beat in the eggs one at a time and add the vanilla essence. Beat in the flour and baking powder. Stir in the date mixture (this will leave you with a runny mixture). Pour into a greased ovenproof dish and bake at 200°C for 40 minutes, until the sponge springs back up when pressed. While the pudding is baking, make the toffee sauce.

Place all ingredients in a pan, combine and bring to the boil for three minutes.

When the pudding is cooked, prick with a skewer several times, then pour over the toffee sauce. Serve immediately with custard, cream or ice cream.

I heard of one restaurant proprietor whose idea of sticky toffee pudding is as follows: Cut a Jamaica ginger cake into slices. Place one on each plate and cover with sauce. There's no substitute for the genuine article.

I.R.

Squidgy chocolate pudding with white chocolate and orange sauce

These puddings are suitable for coeliacs as ground almonds are used in place of flour.

INGREDIENTS

Squidgy chocolate pudding:

125g best quality dark chocolate, broken into pieces
125g butter
3 large eggs
150g caster sugar
350g ground almonds

White chocolate and
orange sauce:

400g white chocolate, broken into small pieces
300ml double cream
Juice and zest of an orange
2 tsp Cointreau

METHOD

Chocolate pudding:

Grease six 150ml pudding basins with butter. Put the chocolate and butter in a bowl and put over a pan of simmering water, stirring occasionally until melted.

In another bowl beat together the sugar, ground almonds and eggs. Gradually beat in the chocolate mixture.

Pour mixture into the basins until about two-thirds full and cover with pleated foil. Place basins in a pan and pour boiling water in the pan until about two-thirds of the way up the basins. Steam for 40 minutes.

White chocolate and orange sauce:

Heat cream, orange juice and zest gently in a pan. Remove from the heat and add the chocolate, stir until this has melted. Add the Cointreau and serve with the pudding and crème fraiche.

The white chocolate sauce will keep in a fridge for ten days and is delicious served warmed and poured over vanilla ice cream.

Vanilla parfait with brandy snap

INGREDIENTS

You will need for the
Vanilla parfait:

600ml milk
1 vanilla pod
Drop of vanilla extract
400g caster sugar
300g pasteurised egg yolk
1 tsp corn flour
750ml double cream

Brandy snaps:

100g butter
100g sugar
100g golden syrup
100g plain flour
1tsp ground ginger

METHOD

To make the parfait, heat the milk, vanilla pod and extract gently in a pan to infuse. Mix together 300g of the caster sugar with egg yolk and corn flour. Add hot milk, stir and then return to the pan. Cook mixture until it thickens. Chill mixture. Whip cream and remaining 100g caster sugar to a soft peak. Fold into chilled custard mixture. Line two loaf tins with cling film and divide mixture between tins. Wrap well with cling film and place in freezer to set.

Brandy snaps:

Melt together the butter and sugar in a pan. Stir in the syrup, flour and ginger and mix well. Spoon the mixture into small heaps onto a baking sheet, leaving large spaces between each heap. Place into a preheated oven at 180°C and bake for 7 to 8 minutes. To roll the brandy snaps, wrap each one around a wooden spoon handle and press together at the join. Allow to cool before serving with slices of parfait and summer berries of your choice.

The parfait keeps well in the freezer. Prepare it ahead for your dinner party, along with the brandy snaps, which should be stored in an airtight container. All you have to do is assemble the dish when you're ready.

P.G.

Yorkshire curd tart

INGREDIENTS

For the pastry:

200g plain flour
50g icing sugar
100g butter
Pinch of salt
1 egg, beaten

To make the filling:

200g curd cheese
50g golden caster sugar
2 eggs, beaten
50g currants (soaked in 2 tblsp
rum overnight)
25g melted butter
Finely grated rind of half a lemon
Good pinch of freshly grated
nutmeg

METHOD

Pastry:
Preheat oven to 200°c. Mix flour, salt and icing sugar
in a bowl, then rub in diced butter until it resembles
breadcrumbs. Add the egg and mix to a smooth
consistency. Roll out and line an 18cm tart tin. Leave
to rest.

Filling:
Mix cheese, sugar, lemon, beaten eggs and melted
butter. Stir in the currants.

Prick the pastry case, and then fill with the mixture.
Grate nutmeg over the top and then bake for approx
40 - 50 minutes until the top is golden.

This delicious tart is a Yorkshire classic. For me it's unbeatable
with Wensleydale cheese and a pint of ale. If you cannot get hold
of curd cheese you can easily make your own. To make 200g, bring
to the boil two pints of full cream milk. As it comes to the boil,
turn off the heat and stir in 2 tsps of Epsom salts. The milk will
separate. Pour mixture through a sieve and you will be left with
the curd cheese.

I. R.

Magpie fuffle slice

INGREDIENTS

250g dark cooking chocolate
200g softened butter
200g caster sugar
2 eggs
2 handfuls sultanas
2 handfuls chopped mixed nuts
1 handful glace cherries
400g dessicated coconut

METHOD

Grease and line a swiss roll tin with baking parchment. Melt the chocolate and pour into the tin, smooth until even thickness and allow to set.

Place the butter and sugar in a bowl and beat well until light and fluffy. Beat in the eggs then mix in the sultanas, nuts and cherries. Add the coconut to the mixture, half at a time.

Push the mixture down onto the chocolate, and then bake at 160 - 170°c for 1 hour, until golden. Allow to cool and then cut into slices, serve with whipped cream, grated chocolate and fresh fruit.

It's wheat free - great for those with special dietary needs. And for everyone else come to that, as it's one of the most popular desserts.

P.G.

Lemon meringue pot

INGREDIENTS

For the lemon curd:

225g caster sugar
225g unsalted butter
Finely-grated zest and juice of 3 lemons
5 egg yolks

For the meringues:

5 egg whites
250g caster sugar

METHOD

Put the sugar, butter, lemon juice and zest into a bowl and stir over a pan of simmering water. When the butter has melted and the sugar has dissolved, beat in the egg yolks and continue to cook for 20 minutes until the curd thickens. Pour into a clean jar and allow to cool.

Meringues:

Preheat oven to 130°c. Line two baking trays with non-stick baking parchment.

Whisk the egg whites to soft peak. Add the sugar a little at a time and whisk until firm. Spoon heaps of the mixture onto baking sheets and cook in the oven for two hours. Turn the oven off and leave the meringues to cool.

To make the lemon pot, mix equal quantities of lemon curd and mascarpone cheese (half jar curd to a 250g tub mascarpone). Layer mixture in a cup or glass with crushed meringues. Serve with whipped cream and shortbread.

Any leftover curd can be kept in the fridge for up to 2 weeks and is delicious on toast. Leftover meringues keep for a long time in an airtight container.

A nice twist on a dessert reminiscent of the seventies - I.R.
Wouldn't know Ian, it was before my time - P.G.
You're fired - I.R.

Diabetic cake

INGREDIENTS

750g sultanas
150g ready-to-use dried apricots, chopped
300ml pineapple juice
1 tsp almond essence
1 tsp nutmeg
1 tsp cinnamon
250g butter
1 cup black tea
(Place all these ingredients in a pan and stir over heat until the butter has melted. Leave to soak overnight)
3 eggs
250g self-raising flour
250g wholemeal flour

METHOD

Grease and line two deep 18cm cake tins. Preheat oven to 160°C.

Beat the eggs into the soaked mixture, and then mix in the flours. Divide mixture between the tins and bake for 1 hour 15 minutes, or until a skewer comes out clean.

This cake freezes very well if desired. Simply cut the cake into portions, wrap and freeze, then defrost portions as required.

Serve with a good sized wedge of mature cheddar.

"The restaurant business has had to quickly adapt to cater for those with special dietary needs and indeed we at The Magpie have always believed in making good simple well-cooked food accessible to all. Despite its name, this cake is pretty good whether you are diabetic or not. That's because we believe special needs dishes shouldn't be like taking your medicine - they should be enjoyable in their own right.

I.R.

Profiteroles with dark chocolate sauce

INGREDIENTS

For the profiteroles:
125g butter
150g plain flour
4 medium eggs
300ml water

For the dark chocolate sauce
375g dark chocolate
2 tblsp golden syrup
175ml double cream
60ml milk

For the pastry cream filling:
2 eggs
100g caster sugar
50g plain flour
1/2litre milk
Vanilla essence
200ml whipping cream

METHOD

Preheat the oven (220°c, gas 8). Heat the water and butter in a pan. When the butter has melted bring to a rolling boil. Add the flour and beat into a smooth thick paste. Remove from the pan, place into a bowl and cool slightly. Lightly beat the eggs and add, a little at a time, to the paste, beating well each time to form a very thick batter. Place the mixture into a piping bag and pipe small balls, about half the size of a golf ball, onto a baking tray lined with parchment. Sprinkle the tray with water and bake for 20 to 25 minutes or until puffed and golden.

To make the sauce - heat the cream and milk in a pan. Remove from the heat and add the chocolate and golden syrup. Stir until the chocolate has melted.

To make the filling - whisk the eggs and sugar together until almost white. Meanwhile bring the milk to the boil and then whisk into the egg and sugar mixture. Return the mixture to the pan and bring back to the boil, stirring until it thickens. Remove from the heat and add a drop of vanilla essence. Allow the mixture to cool prior to use. Whip 200ml whipping cream and then mix in equal quantities with the pastry cream. Transfer cream to a piping bag. Make a small hole in each profiterole with your finger and pipe cream mixture into each one. Arrange on a plate and top with warm dark chocolate sauce.

The dark chocolate sauce will keep in a fridge for ten days and is delicious served warmed and poured over vanilla ice cream.

P.G.

Vanilla pannacotta with poached rhubarb

INGREDIENTS

1 litre double cream
300ml milk
100g caster sugar
1 tblsp vanilla extract
8 leaves of gelatine
2 vanilla pods
1.5kg rhubarb
150g granulated sugar
1 vanilla pod

METHOD

Slowly heat the cream, milk, caster sugar and vanilla pods (split length ways, seeds scraped out and put into the cream) do not boil the cream. Soak the gelatine in cold water until it becomes soft and add it to the cream to dissolve. Remove the vanilla pods and pour the cream into dishes. Chill.

Wash and trim the rhubarb removing any tough skin and cut into 2cm pieces at an angle to give a diamond shape. Place it into a pan with the sugar and vanilla pod (split and the seeds scraped out and put in with the rhubarb). Bring to the boil over a low heat and cook for two minutes or until the rhubarb is tender but not fallen. Remove from the heat, remove the pod and chill.

To serve, take each dish of pannacotta and add a good spoonful of rhubarb and serve.

For a delicious white chocolate pannacotta (perfect with poached summer berries or orange and raisin cookies), leave out the vanilla pods and sugar and replace them with 150g of white chocolate. Paul grimaces when I say this, but I reckon this dessert is perfect with a glass of Asti. Funny lads, these chefs. To enjoy the dish at its best, go for the early rhubarb in July and August.

I. R.

Summer berries with warm white chocolate sauce

INGREDIENTS

1kg fresh soft berries
(we suggest:
250g strawberries
150g raspberries
150g blueberries
150g blackcurrants
150g redcurrants
150g blackberries)
250g white chocolate
250ml double cream
1 tsp vanilla extract

METHOD

Hull and thoroughly wash all the berries and divide them into dessert bowls. To make the sauce, heat the cream and add it to the chocolate with the vanilla and mix thoroughly. Pour the warm sauce over the berries, garnish with a sprig of fresh mint and serve immediately.

For a variation on the sauce, add the zest and juice of half an orange and a tablespoon of Cointreau. Serve with a rich dark chocolate pudding or pour over vanilla ice cream and serve with all butter shortbread.

P.G.

White chocolate and raspberry trifle

INGREDIENTS

16 sponge fingers
1 lb frozen raspberries,
lightly thawed
200ml crème de framboise
100g icing sugar
1 litre custard
500g white chocolate
300ml whipping cream
50g caster sugar
50g crushed hazelnuts

METHOD

Lay sponge fingers in deep dish (approx 6cm deep) and pour over 50ml of crème de framboise. Blitz raspberries, icing sugar and remaining 150ml of the crème de framboise to a puree. Pour the puree over the sponge fingers.

Heat the custard and add white chocolate. Stir until melted. Allow custard to cool slightly and then pour over top of the sponge fingers and puree.

Whip together cream and caster sugar until stiff. Spread over the top of the trifle. Sprinkle with crushed hazelnuts. Chill for at least an hour before serving.

"Its close association with the much-maligned seventies, when it appeared on menus everywhere, has rendered trifle somewhat unfashionable. Not with us.
Tastes great, and there are so many flavour combinations you can try. This is one of the best."

P.G.

Fresh strawberry and hazelnut meringue and strawberry cream

INGREDIENTS

For the meringue:

3 egg whites
180g caster sugar
Pinch of cream of tartar
50g finely crushed hazelnuts

For the
strawberry cream:

100g sugar
50ml water
500g strawberries
2 leaves gelatine
400ml double cream

METHOD

To make the meringue: Whisk egg whites with cream of tartar until soft peak. Add half of the sugar and whisk until stiff and glossy. Fold in the remaining sugar and hazelnuts. Put mixture into a piping bag and pipe into approx 5cm spirals onto a lined baking tray. Cook in a pre-heated oven at 140°c for about an hour. When they feel firm, lift them up to check that the underside is cooked. Turn off the oven and leave the meringues inside until they are cool.

Put the water and sugar in a pan and heat until a light syrup. Cut the strawberries in half (or smaller if large strawberries) and lightly poach in syrup until they are soft. Meanwhile soak the gelatine in cold water.

To make the strawberry cream: Puree the syrup and strawberries. Pass through a sieve into a bowl. Add the gelatine to the warm puree, stir in to disolve and then lightly chill.

Whip the double cream until soft peaks are formed. Fold the puree into the cream. To serve, layer meringues with strawberry cream and thinly sliced strawberries, finishing off with a meringue on top (using three meringues in total). Serve with strawberry coulis (see Extras).

This is a long-standing Magpie favourite. Proof, were it needed, that the customer is always right.

I.R.

Lemon mousse

INGREDIENTS

200ml fresh lemon juice
Zest of 1 lemon
150g caster sugar
4 leaves gelatine
450ml whipping cream
4 large scoops vanilla ice cream
Splash brandy

METHOD

Put the lemon juice, zest and sugar into a pan and heat until sugar has dissolved. Meanwhile soak gelatine in cold water. Add gelatine to lemon mixture and cool slightly. Whip the cream to soft peak, add ice cream and mix slowly. Slowly add lemon mixture and then brandy. Pour into glass dishes and chill for one to two hours before serving with whipped cream.

"This has been on our menu for as long as I have been here. And after 28 years, it's still as popular as ever.
I. R.

Caramelised rice pudding with raspberry jam

INGREDIENTS

125g pudding rice
3 pints milk
1 vanilla pod
1 397g tin condensed milk
1 capful vanilla extract

To serve:
Raspberry jam

To finish:
Demerara sugar

METHOD

Put all ingredients in a pan and bring to the boil. Reduce the heat and simmer until fluffy and creamy, stirring occasionally. Place your favourite raspberry jam in the bottom of a dish and top with rice pudding. Sprinkle with demerara sugar and caramelise by either using a catering blow torch, or by placing under the grill for a few minutes.

A pudding that never fails to evoke memories of schooldays... and proof that things weren't always better in the past. A delicious twist on an old school favourite.

I.R.

Warm chocolate pot with hazelnut macaroon and fruit skewer

INGREDIENTS

Ingredients for the chocolate pot:

300ml double cream
200g dark chocolate, broken into small pieces
2 egg yolks
3 tblsp brandy
20g butter
Drop of vanilla extract

Ingredients for the hazelnut macaroons:

350g caster sugar
250g ground hazelnuts
4 egg whites, lightly whipped

Ingredients for the fruit skewer:

Place a selection of fruits onto a skewer and serve with the chocolate pot and hazelnut macaroon (try strawberries and kiwi).

METHOD

Chocolate pot:
Heat the cream and vanilla extract in a pan until nearly at boiling point. Allow to cool for a minute and add the chocolate. Stir until smooth, and then add the egg yolks and brandy. Return to gentle heat for a few minutes to ensure the egg is cooked stirring continuously. Allow mixture to cool slightly before adding butter and stirring until smooth. Pour mixture into espresso cups and serve immediately with macaroons and a fruit skewer.

Hazelnut macaroons:
Mix together all ingredients. Place small spoonfuls of mixture onto lined baking trays, leaving room for mixture to spread. Bake for 12 minutes at 200°c, the biscuits will harden on cooling.

If you prefer to make the chocolate pots in advance simply store in fridge and heat for a few seconds in microwave prior to serving

"Go on, have a dip!

P.G.

Bananas with butterscotch sauce and fromage frais

INGREDIENTS

6 Fresh bananas
907g tin golden syrup
75g butter
250g light brown sugar
1tblsp vanilla extract
300ml double cream
300ml fromage frais

METHOD

Put the syrup, butter and sugar in a pan and slowly bring to the boil. When it's up to a rolling boil, cook for three minutes, keeping it on the boil. Remove from the heat and cool slightly. Add the vanilla and cream and mix well. Pour into clean jars and leave to cool.

To serve, slice the bananas into a dish and pour over a good spoonful of sauce, finish with fromage frais.

"Make a reasonable quantity of the butterscotch sauce as it goes beautifully with so many other things - drizzle it over ice cream or pancakes or mix with sliced apples and top with an oaty crumble. Mmmm!"

P.G.

Chocolate and hazelnut brownie

INGREDIENTS

300g dark chocolate
200g butter
400g caster sugar
4 eggs
275g plain flour
275g crushed hazelnuts
1 tblsp vanilla essence

METHOD

Melt the butter and chocolate together in a bowl, (either in the microwave or over a bain marie).

Add the sugar, eggs and vanilla essence. Mix well. Sieve the flour and fold into the mixture with the hazelnuts.

Pour the mixture into a 30 x 20cm baking tin lined with baking parchment. Bake at 160°C for 1 hour to 1 hour and 20 minutes. To test if it is cooked put a skewer into the brownie. If it comes out almost clean the brownie is ready (any mixture on the skewer will be sticky but not wet).

"A delightful treat for chocaholics. And our standby at the café if someone suddenly lets us know it's their birthday. During a busy service we can still find time to pop a few candles into a plate of brownies. Just as well our front of house staff can sing!"

I.R.

Extras

THE MAGPIE CAFE

Sauces, sides, dressings & drizzlings

Strawberry coulis

400g fresh strawberries
125ml water
100g caster sugar
Juice of half a lemon

Boil all the ingredients together, allow to cool slightly. Liquidise and strain.

Lime créme fraiche

400g créme fraiche
Juice and zest of 4 limes
Pepper

Simply add the juice and zest of the limes to the créme fraiche with a little pepper. A perfect accompaniment.

Sponge fingers (for trifles)

2 eggs (separated)
50g caster sugar
50g plain flour (sieved)
Icing sugar

Whisk the egg whites until stiff. Cream the egg yolk and sugar until light and fluffy (almost white in colour).

Add a little egg white to the creamed mix to 'cut in'. Gradually add the sieved flour alternating with the remaining egg white, and mixing as lightly as possible.

Put into a piping bag with a plain nozzle and pipe onto a lined baking sheet (in approx 8cm lengths). Sprinkle with icing sugar and rest for five minutes.

Bake at 220°C for approx 10 minutes, or until firm and golden.

Tartare sauce

500g mayonnaise
50g capers
150g gherkins
Juice of 1 lime
1/2 tsp Tabasco sauce
1/2tsp Worcester sauce
1 sprig parsley, chopped
(to give about 1 heaped tsp)

Finely chop the capers, gherkins and parsley. Add to the mayonnaise with the lime juice, Tabasco and Worcester sauce and mix well.

Marie rose sauce

350g mayonnaise
100g salad cream
150g tomato ketchup
1 tsp lemon juice
1 tsp Worcester sauce
1/2 tsp Tabasco sauce

Mix all the ingredients together.

Any unused sauce can be placed in an air tight jar and kept in the fridge for up to one week.

Balsamic dressing

100ml aged balsamic vinegar
100ml extra virgin olive oil
(oils made from kalamata
olives are the best)
Salt and pepper

Mix the oil, vinegar, salt
and pepper together by
shaking vigorously until
they emulsify. Season to
taste.

Horseradish dressing

2 tblsp mayonnaise
1 tblsp horseradish sauce
1-2 tblsp water
Freshly milled black pepper

Mix the mayonnaise and
horseradish together. Add
enough water so the
dressing is not too stiff.
Check the seasoning and
adjust to taste.

This dressing will keep for
up to five days in the
fridge.

Fish stock

1kg fish bones
1 large onion
1 leek (white part only)
1 stick celery
1/2 lemon
2-3 parsley stalks
3-4 white peppercorns
1 bay leaf
30g butter
2 1/2 litres water

Sweat (cook without colour)
the vegetables and bones in
the butter for about five
minutes. Add the bay leaf,
peppercorns, lemon, parsley
and water. Bring to the boil,
skimming if necessary. Reduce
heat to a rapid simmer for 20
minutes.

Sieve the stock, pass through
some muslin and chill.

Recipe Index

ISBN 0-9549254-0-8